The GOSPEL *in the* PIANO KEYBOARD?

The GOSPEL *in the* PIANO KEYBOARD?

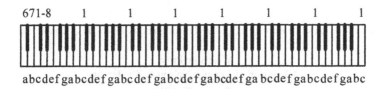

671-8   1   1   1   1   1   1   1

abcdef gabcdef gabc def gabcdef gabcdef ga bcdef gabcdef gabc

A Study of the Spiritual Meanings
of Certain Numbers in the Scriptures and How
They Help Understand Prophecy

RAYMOND CHRISTENSON

WESTBOW
P R E S S®
A DIVISION OF THOMAS NELSON
& ZONDERVAN

This book is a work of non-fiction. Unless otherwise noted, the author and the publisher make no explicit guarantees as to the accuracy of the information contained in this book and in some cases, names of people and places have been altered to protect their privacy.

Scripture quotations taken from the New American Standard Bible®, Copyright © 1960, 1962, 1963, 1968, 1971, 1972, 1973, 1975, 1977, 1995 by The Lockman Foundation. Used by permission. (www.Lockman.org)

Scripture taken from the King James Version of the Bible.

WestBow Press books may be ordered through booksellers or by contacting:

WestBow Press
A Division of Thomas Nelson & Zondervan
1663 Liberty Drive
Bloomington, IN 47403
www.westbowpress.com
1 (866) 928-1240

ISBN: 978-1-4908-9658-8 (sc)
ISBN: 978-1-4908-9659-5 (hc)
ISBN: 978-1-4908-9657-1 (e)

Library of Congress Control Number: 2015911305

Print information available on the last page.

WestBow Press rev. date: 07/29/2015

This writing is intended to be a simple testimony
of spiritual things heard from the Scriptures by
Ray Christenson.
rc7keyboard@yahoo.com

Preface

671-8

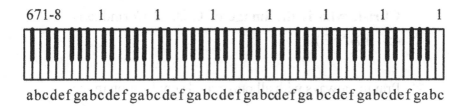

abcdefgabcdefgabcdefgabcdefgabcdefga bcdefgabcdefgabc

God's Redemption Plan and the Piano Keyboard

Question: Did those responsible for establishing the system of recording musical sounds use the gospel as the foundation for their work?

The *Encyclopedia of Americana* says the following in regard to music: "The ultimate origins of the art of organizing sounds are too remote in time to be determined accurately." The Lord, of course, would have been present no matter how remote in time. Be aware that this writer pleads total ignorance to the history of music theory, confesses to very little knowledge of music theory, and certainly does not fully understand the answer to this question. The parallel between the numerical organization of the gospel and musical sounds surely could not have happened by chance. Yes, there are other forms of keyboards, but this keyboard is the one that will be used to outline this writing because of its numerical organization.

Listen as you read these Scriptures:

And even if our gospel is veiled, **it is veiled** to those who are perishing, in whose case the god of this world has blinded the minds of the unbelieving, that they might not see the light of the gospel of the glory of **Christ, who is the image** of God. (2 Corinthians 4:3–4 NASB)

Praying always with all prayer and supplication in the Spirit, and watching thereunto with all perseverance and supplication for all saints; And for me, that utterance may be given unto me, that I may open my mouth boldly, to make known the **mystery** of the gospel. (Ephesians 6:18–19 KJV)

Behold, I shew you **a mystery**; We shall not all sleep, but we shall all be changed, 52 In a moment, in the twinkling of an eye, at the last trump: for the trumpet shall sound, and the dead shall be raised incorruptible, and **we shall be changed.** (1 Corinthians 15:51–52 KJV)

But their minds were hardened; for until this very day at the reading of the old covenant the same **veil remains unlifted, because it is removed in Christ.** But to this day whenever Moses is read, a veil lies over their heart; but whenever a man turns to the Lord, the **veil is taken away.** Now the Lord is the Spirit; and where the Spirit of the Lord is, there is liberty. But we all, with unveiled face beholding as in a mirror the glory of the Lord, are being transformed into the same image from glory to glory, just as from the Lord, the Spirit. (2 Corinthians 3:14–18 NASB)

What a blessing when we experience the unveiling of spiritual truths as the image of our Lord Jesus becomes more and more a part of our lives. At some point, while the Lord was unveiling certain spiritual truths of the gospel, this writer began to notice that certain fundamental elements of the gospel appeared in the core elements of music as observed on the piano keyboard.

Question: Do you have an ear for music?

That ear is a God-given talent with which some folks have been blessed from the moment they were born.

The more important question: Has God, through His Holy Spirit, given you an ear that unveils the good news of our Lord Jesus? God gives this ear to all when they accept Jesus as Savior by faith and are then born again with the second spiritual birth. With this ear we hear in part. The Scripture assures us that on that day when "we shall be changed," then we will know the rest of the story. Walking by the piano repeatedly and not seeing the gospel is not a problem. Reading through the Scripture repeatedly and not hearing the gospel can be a problem.

Question: Do you want to play the piano?

This writing is a simple testimony of certain spiritual truths heard from God's holy Word. This writer shared with a precious brother in the Lord how God unveiled certain truths as to the season of the second coming of our Lord—and asked the question "Should I write a book on these second-coming Scriptures?" The friend's reply: "Yes, but [that was a qualified yes] first write a book on the spiritual meaning of numbers." This writer was, at that point, unaware that the spiritual meanings of certain numbers had been unveiled and had become foundational to the understanding of certain Scriptures that are part of God's redemption plan.

The goal of this writing, then, is simply to first share the spiritual meaning of certain <u>numbers</u> from the gospel, using the keyboard of the piano as the outline, and then apply these spiritual meanings to certain Scriptures pertaining to knowledge of the season of the Lord's return.

Remember as you read that this writing is all about the <u>redemption plan</u> of God. The season of the Lord's return is part of that redemption plan. You may also find it necessary to read a great deal of this writing before the numerical organization of the keyboard begins to parallel the numerical organization of the gospel.

Many Scriptures are included in this writing to present the various ways that the Lord has chosen to unveil His redemption plan. Understanding how God communicated His plan throughout the Old Testament becomes foundational to understanding John's prophecy, as much of his writing in the book of Revelation is symbolism from those Scriptures. Observing and then understanding certain numbers that the Lord has entrenched in numerous Scriptures will certainly help make the transition from the literal to the spiritual dimension of the gospel.

The Lord speaks through His Scriptures, so listen carefully as the Scriptures are read. May the Lord bless you abundantly as you reflect <u>in the Spirit</u> on the Scriptures presented within the pages of this study.

1

671-8   1   1   1   1   1   1   1

b c d e f g a b c d e f g a b c d e f g a b c d e f g a b c d e f g a b c d e f g a b c d e f g a b c
A

Play this A as the sixth day of the week.

Seven notes—white keys A through G—are arranged on the keyboard to total fifty-two. That is the same number as the number of days from the cross to Pentecost. The first A represents Friday, the day our precious Lord and Savior became the perfect sacrifice for the sin of all who have invited Him into their lives by faith. The sixth day, Friday, was the day Jesus was crucified on the cross and is where the fifty-two days begin.

> **But this man, after he had offered one sacrifice for sins for ever**, sat down on the right hand of God; From henceforth expecting till his enemies be made his footstool. For by one offering he hath perfected for ever them that are sanctified. (Hebrews 10:12–14 KJV)

Why was it significant that the Lord was crucified on the sixth day in God's redemption plan? A review of the creation account is where it all begins and then explains the significance of the sixth day.

Physical Life Created on the Sixth Day

The Bible begins with these words: "In the beginning." It was during that period of time known as the sixth day of the week that it all began for man and woman. That is, in the evening, man did not exist, and in the morning, Adam and Eve were created on the <u>sixth</u> day or at the beginning of the sixth period of time of the creation account. It was the <u>eighth</u> proclamation, "**then God said**," on the sixth day when man and woman were created. The salvation of all believers will be complete when the sign of the eighth day Sabbath rest will be completed at the second coming of our Lord, which identifies with the eighth proclamation. This book uses the term "eighth day" to refer to eternal life after the second coming of our Lord, as the all the redeemed will then experience the literal rest of God. The eighth day follows the seven periods that the Lord used in the Scriptures as a timeline, from the beginning of the second captivity of Israel and ending when the Lord appears to take up His church.

> And the LORD God formed man of the dust of the ground, and breathed into his nostrils **the breath of life;** and man became a living soul. (Genesis 2:7 KJV)

The writer of the book of Revelation uses this same phrase "<u>the breath of life</u>," as it appears in the first Scripture (Genesis 2:7), to describe the physical resurrection of the saints at the end of the age. This Scripture teaches that Adam's and Eve's bodies were made from the elements of this earth. The breath of life that came from God

2

resulted in man, generally known as body, spirit, and soul. Genesis 1:26 presents man as created in the image and likeness of God the Father, God the Son, and God the Holy Spirit. The word "likeness" brings to mind Galatians 5:22–23. That is, it is the nature of the Godhead to manifest love, joy, peace, patience, kindness, goodness, faithfulness, gentleness, and self-control. Likeness, of course, can mean much more than the fruit of the Spirit. The phrase "eternal life" comes to mind.

The Image of God Added to the Physical Life of Mankind

Adam and Eve created in God's image:

> **And God said**, Let us make man in **our image**, after our likeness: and let them have dominion over the fish of the sea, and over the fowl of the air, and over the cattle, and over all the earth, and over every creeping thing that creepeth upon the earth. So God created man in **his own image**, in the image of God created he him; **male and female** created he them. ... And God saw everything that he had made, and, behold, it was very good. And the evening and the morning were **the sixth day.** (Genesis 1:26–27, 31 KJV)

Eternal spiritual life, however, may be better understood by the word "image." In Genesis 1:27 the Scripture narrows the image from "our" to "His." Adam and Eve then were created in the spiritual image of God. Remember, God is Spirit. *Tselem*[1] is the Hebrew word translated as "image" in this verse. It means to shade, as a phantom or a representative figure.

3

Listen as you read:

God is a Spirit: and they that worship him must worship him in spirit and in truth. (John 4:24 KJV)

Be aware that in the Scriptures, man created in the image of God appears in the creation account of Adam, Eve, and the birth of our Lord Jesus. The only other Scripture is Genesis 9:6, where it is used as the goal of God's redemption plan in the covenant between God and Noah.

The Holy Spirit, joined to the spirits of Adam and Eve, allowed them to enter the seventh-day rest and partake of the provision of God in the garden. God must be present for His image to be manifested in the lives of those who have chosen to be saved.

Jesus created in the image of God:

Listen as you read:

Jesus saith unto him, Have I been so long time with you, and yet hast thou not known me, Philip? **he that hath seen me hath seen the Father**; and how sayest thou then, Shew us the Father? (John 14:9 KJV)

When we look at Jesus, we see the image of God. Jesus was born of a virgin and was conceived by God. Jesus, in his humanity, then was born not separated from God or the same as Adam and Eve were created. Jesus did not sin when tempted. Adam and Eve sinned and were separated from the image of God.

4

The chosen saved are transformed into God's image. The references to all those who are saved is that we are conformed to the image of Jesus.

Read:

> But we all, with unveiled face beholding as in a mirror the glory of the Lord, are being **transformed into the same image** from glory to glory, just as from the Lord, the Spirit. (2 Corinthians 3:18 NASB)

When we look in the mirror, we see our image.

And again:

> And just as **we have borne the image of the earthy**, we shall also bear **the image of the heavenly.** (1 Corinthians 15:49 NASB)

The fact that God's precious Holy Spirit can and must be joined to man's spirit surely is the defining spiritual truth from the creation story of man. This simply sets man apart from the rest of God's creation. The Scriptures teach that God is eternal. Eternal life then can only be attained by His image being present in our lives. All of mankind has and will be born with the fallen-sin nature inherited from the sin of Adam and Eve. All must be born again with the spiritual birth to receive the image of God.

Listen as you read:

If he set his heart upon man, if he gather <u>unto himself</u> **his** <u>spirit and</u> **his** <u>breath</u>; All flesh shall perish together, and man **shall turn again unto dust.** (Job 34:14–15 KJV)

The Origin of Sin

But of the fruit of the tree which is in the midst of the garden, God hath said, Ye shall not eat of it, neither shall <u>ye touch it</u>, lest ye **die**. And the serpent said unto the woman, Ye shall not surely die. (Genesis 3:3–4 KJV)

Solomon shared with us that it is pure insanity to choose any other path than the one the Lord has prepared for us. Think about it. Adam and Eve had any and all good things from which to choose. They had freedom to choose from all that God had prepared for them. They didn't have to deal with evil and in fact didn't even have knowledge of evil until after they had eaten from the tree of knowledge of good and evil. Man served God and one another instead of exploiting each other. They only had to choose to keep God the <u>Lord</u> of their lives by not even touching that tree.

And when the woman saw that the tree was good for food, and that it was pleasant to the eyes, and a tree to be desired to make one wise, <u>she took of the fruit thereof, and did eat</u>, and gave also unto her husband with her; and <u>he did eat.</u> (Genesis 3:6 KJV)

6

The lies of the Devil seemed logical to them, instead of God's instruction, and they made the wrong decision. They disobeyed God. Remember, they did not have the fallen nature that we are born with when they made this choice. The first indication in the creation story that God was separated from them comes after they had sinned, for it says, "He came to them." The fact that Adam and Eve's sin resulted in all mankind being born with a carnal nature <u>separated</u> from God is the one central truth we must understand as we follow the presentation of God's redemption plan on the keyboard. This fallen nature is, in fact, understood in some detail, as we live in a world filled with the carnal or fallen nature of man. The problem we have is making the transition from our fallen carnal nature to our new spiritual nature, which is received by faith through the new birth; that is, the baptism of the Holy Spirit. Jesus gave us certain insight, as we observe His life, as to what to expect when we are changed at the bodily resurrection. Jesus was born through the virgin birth without a sinful nature; that is, He, in His humanity, was never separated from God until that moment on the cross when He took on all our sins and sacrificed Himself for us. The good news, of course, is that Jesus had no sin of His own and no fallen carnal nature, so the grave could not hold Him.

Certain Results of Being Separated from God by Sin

A country preacher was once quoted as saying, "You have to get them lost before you can get them saved." He, of course, was saying that the Holy Spirit first convicts of sin before repentance can result in forgiveness and redemption. A vision of the lost state of mankind is also necessary to understand why redemption is necessary. The transition from the lost state of being **to the state**

7

of being of the seventh-day rest becomes extremely exciting when knowledge gained is added to what the Holy Spirit makes known to all believers at the new birth. The Lord has given us the Bible to help us understand the differences between the lost state of being and the saved state of being.

The good news is that the redeemed have received a new spiritual nature though the new birth. The bad news is that this fallen or carnal nature will still be with us until we are changed, when we go to be with the Lord. This carnal body and carnal nature will be taken away at that time. Our spiritual nature will be joined with a new spiritual body when our salvation is complete. The Scripture tells us that there is <u>a way that seems right to our carnal nature</u>.

> There is a way which seemeth right unto a man, but the end thereof are the ways of death. (Proverbs 14:12 KJV)

Removing what seems right is what the sanctification process is all about. The Lord simply wants all of these things out of our lives. Sometimes making the right choice to remove sin from our lives is like going to the dentist to have a tooth pulled. We know we need to do it, but we don't want to do it. Sometimes we are unaware of what needs to be done. The following is a list of certain things that resulted from the sin of Adam. It's a short list, so remember to ask the Lord for His long list. This list will be revisited in the chapter on Pentecost.

Separated from God's Righteousness

The Bible defines the state of being of both the unrighteousness and the righteousness. The words "unrighteousness" and "unrighteous" appear thirty-three times in the Bible. The words "righteous" and "righteousness" appear a total of 609 times in the Scriptures. Separation from God has separated man from God's righteousness. The result, of course, is a form of self-righteousness that manifests from the carnal nature of man. The law of God gives us a perfect example of the difference between self-righteousness and God's righteousness. The reason for the law was to define sin.

Listen as you read this Scripture:

> What shall we say then? Is the law sin? God forbid. Nay, <u>I had not known sin, but by the law</u>: for I had not known lust, except the law had said, Thou shalt not covet. (Romans 7:7 KJV)

Knowing the law and keeping it are two different things. One cannot keep the law out of one's self-righteousness and have it result in a righteousness that is acceptable to God. That separation must be first bridged by faith in our Lord. It does not come naturally for the carnal nature of man to understand <u>what the lost state of the sixth-day state of being is all about</u>. God gave the law in the form of the Ten Commandments to identify what sin is and what it means to be lost. Look around and notice that the world separated from God does not get it. Remember, one's conscience can be trained.

Listen as you read this Scripture:

> And be found in him, <u>not having mine own righteousness</u>, which is of the law, but that which is through the faith of Christ, **the righteousness which is of God by faith.** (Philippians 3:9 KJV)

Separated from the Provision of God in the Garden

Therefore the LORD God sent him forth from the garden of Eden, to till the ground from whence he was taken. So he drove out the man; and he placed at the east of the garden of Eden Cherubims, and a flaming sword which turned every way, to keep the way of the tree of life. (Genesis 3:23–24 KJV)

The eighty-hour workweek began, later reduced to forty hours, and now is headed back up toward the eighty-hour mark. It's as if the world simply does not get it. No problem; I'll just get a bigger barn and compete with those around me, and fill it up and I'll be fine. It will be embarrassing for all of us when we stand before the Lord and try to explain why we just didn't just trust Him in everything. Mankind's trying to make provision for themselves has not worked out that well in history. Being separated from God's provision completely changes everything, yet the world is not aware that God's provision is available to all who believe and are led by the Spirit. Works separated from God are not the same as works resulting from a faith relationship with God.

Separated from the Seventh-Day Rest

Keep in mind that the seventh-day rest represents the spiritual state of being into which the redeemed can enter by faith. This state of being will become literal when we enter the eighth-day period after we are changed at the resurrection, when the Lord returns. Remember that in the creation account, the seventh day has no beginning or end. There was no evening and morning connected to the seventh day. Remember that Adam and Eve were created in His image first and then allowed to enter the seventh-day rest. They were not only removed by sin from the garden, but they also were removed and separated from the seventh-day rest.

> For if **Joshua** had given them rest, He would not have
> spoken of another day after that. (Hebrews 4:8 NASB)

Joshua was a type of the Lord as they entered into the Holy Land at the end of the first captivity of Israel, yet until the penalty of sin was paid on the cross, the state of being of the seventh-day rest was judicially not available to the redeemed. The world is simply separated from knowledge and experience of the seventh-day rest. Only the redeemed by faith can enter the state of being of the seventh-day rest of God.

Separated from God's Kingdom

Israel asked for a civil government like the world around them had developed. They got it with instructions as to how it would be structured.

> Then all the elders of Israel gathered themselves
> together, and came to Samuel unto Ramah, And said
> unto him, Behold, thou art old, and thy sons walk not
> in thy ways: now make us a king to judge us like all
> the nations. But the thing displeased Samuel, when
> they said, Give us a king to judge us. And Samuel
> prayed unto the LORD. And the LORD said unto
> Samuel, Hearken unto the voice of the people in all

that they say unto thee: for they have not rejected thee, **but they have rejected me, that I should not reign over them.** (1 Samuel 8:4–7 KJV)

The result of Israel's request for a civil government:

And ye shall **cry out** in that day because of your king which ye shall have chosen you; **and the LORD will not hear you in that day.** (1 Samuel 8:18 KJV)

The world continues to cry out, even if you haven't noticed. Does this Scripture mean that as long as mankind continues to look to the political process for answers, the Lord will not hear their prayers? Good grief! Probably the biggest surprise awaiting the redeemed—after the return of the Lord and we are all changed—will be the absence of civil government, for Christ's spiritual kingdom will have become literal. Being governed by the Spirit of God—that was and is God's plan.

Separated from the Perfect Unchanging Language

Mankind separated from the Spirit of God has resulted in being separated from the original language that communicates all spiritual things. Historians of the Bible tell us that the original language was used for some 1,800 years from the creation of man, before the Tower of Babel account of God's judgment came on the use of the original language. Mankind was able to communicate with great unity during that period. One only has to observe, however, how the redemption plan of God was communicated during that period to realize that communication of spiritual things was affected, even though some form of the original language was present.

> Now the whole earth used the **same** language and the **same** words. (Genesis 11:1 NASB)

> Jesus Christ the **same** yesterday, and to day, and for ever. (Hebrews 13:8 KJV)

> And the LORD said, Behold, the people is one, and they have all one language; and this they begin to do: and **now nothing** will be restrained from them, which they have imagined to do. (Genesis 11:6 KJV)

Unity and power existed in and through the original language.

> Go to, let us go down, and there **confound their language**, that they may not understand one another's speech. (Genesis 11:7 KJV)

It does not say that the Lord created new languages but that He confused the language. The biblical record seems quite clear that the language of heaven has not changed. Only the languages that manifest from the carnal nature of man are under a state of constant evolution. We only have to be aware of the dictionary that we use, no matter which language of this world we use. The meaning of each word is in a constant state of change. There is one language that communicates perfectly, and that is the language of heaven.

How God can communicate using the language of heaven to all the divisions of the language at the same time is not understood. One answer received is that God is God, and He can do all things. That's probably as good an answer as could be given. Man was separated from the perfect language, but the good news is that by faith, the Lord provides a way that we might communicate freely with Him without knowledge of how He does it. Keep in mind that angels are involved, communicating God's message throughout the Scriptures. One God who listens and speaks to all the redeemed, angels, and all His creation at the same time is impossible for this writer to understand. Praise the Lord—one doesn't need this knowledge to communicate with God.

Separation from God Resulted in Divorce Being Allowed in the Marriage between Man and Woman

The Bible describes the condition that destroys marriage as "hardness of heart."

> He saith unto them, Moses because of the hardness of your hearts suffered you to put away your wives: **but from the beginning it was not so.** (Matthew 19:8 KJV)

The relationship in marriage between man and woman was created to bring forth physical life. The new-birth relationship between man and God was created to bring forth eternal spiritual life. The marriage relationship is used throughout the Scriptures as a sign to the world of a personal relationship that the redeemed have with God. Adultery has become a sign to the world of separation from God and can destroy the marriage and the witness of the marriage.

14

The Holy Spirit is simply not present in the life of those separated from God by sin to help maintain the marriage relationship.

The Sixth Day Became Synonymous with the Lost or Separated-from-God State of Being of Mankind

The sixth-day period in the creation story has a beginning and an end. God's work ended at the end of the sixth period of time, but the experience of the creation of mankind continues and will <u>end at the end of the age</u>.

> And God saw everything that he had made, and, behold, it was very good. And the evening and the morning **were the sixth day.** (Genesis 1:31 KJV)

God finished His work on the sixth day of the week. His works have been finished from the foundation of the world, yet the redeemed have, can, and will enter into those works until the Lord returns.

> Blessed be the God and Father of our Lord Jesus Christ, who hath blessed us with all spiritual blessings in heavenly places in Christ: According as **he hath chosen us in him before the foundation of the world,** that we should be holy and without blame before him in love. (Ephesians 1:3–4 KJV)

God has a plan for <u>every</u> life that has been chosen to be redeemed by accepting Jesus as their personal Savior. That plan was worked out from the foundation of the world.

The sixth-day state of being for the redeemed will end when the sixth trumpet of the seventh seal of Revelation is complete. When that seventh trumpet—the last trumpet—sounds, the redeemed will be caught up to be with the Lord. Those who have not been born again will be separated from God for eternity. The history of the lost state of being of mankind is summed up by John in the book of Revelation with the use of the three sixes. These will be explained later in this writing. Man was created on the sixth day of the week. The Passover occurred on the sixth day of the week. Jesus went to the cross on Friday the sixth day of the week. The Lord will return at the end of the events of the sixth trumpet of the seventh seal of the book of Revelation.

Everyone except Jesus has been born consistent with the events of the sixth day of creation. That is, God continues to create mankind with a body, spirit, and soul. Jesus said, "Ye must be born again." Mankind is born into this earth separated from the Holy Spirit and is lost for eternity without the second spiritual birth. The carnal, fallen nature inherited from the sin of Adam has been destined to manifest sins at some point by all. Romans 3:23 makes it quite clear that "all have sinned." Recognizing the lost state of being that has been manifested in one's life is the more important issue, so that a faith relationship with the Lord can be chosen, which will manifest with the cleansing of all sin.

Notice as the Scriptures are read that the **number six always refers or points to the lost state of being of mankind** in one manner or another, as everyone is born through the physical birth, separated from the Holy Spirit.

Sixth Day of Redemption

Jesus was crucified at the <u>sixth</u> hour on Friday, the <u>sixth</u> day of the week.

> Now from the <u>sixth hour</u> there was darkness over all the land unto the ninth hour. And about the ninth hour Jesus cried with a loud voice, saying, Eli, Eli, lama sabachthani? that is to say, My God, my God, why hast thou forsaken me? (Matthew 27:45–46 KJV)

> And he bearing his cross went forth into a place called the place of a skull, which is called in the Hebrew Golgotha: Where they crucified him, and two other with him, on either side one, and Jesus in the midst. And Pilate wrote a title, and put it on the cross. And the writing was JESUS OF NAZARETH THE KING OF THE JEWS. (John 19:17–19 KJV)

Think about it. The Lord worked it out that the prophecy of the Passover sign of Israel did happen on the sixth day of the week, or Friday. The Scriptures refer to the Feast of the Passover as an appointed time. Yes, Jesus was predestined to the cross on the sixth day of the week to redeem all found in the sixth-day state of being of the lost. Have you moved from the state of being of the sixth day into the seventh-day rest?

Listen as you read this Scripture:

> **If we confess our sins, he is faithful and just to forgive us our sins, and to cleanse us from all**

unrighteousness. If we say that we have not sinned, we make him a liar, and his word is not in us. (1 John 1:9–10 KJV)

Confess your sins and by faith invite Jesus into your heart, and receive the miracle of the birth.

2

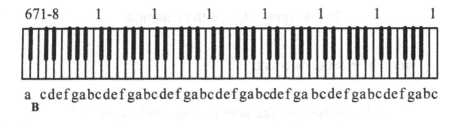

a cdefgabcdefgabcdefgabcdefgabcdefga bcdefgabcdefgabc
B

Play this B as the seventh day of the week.

Why does music have seven notes, A to G? Maybe an answer to this question will take form by reviewing what is known from the Scriptures. Consider first this question: why does the solar calendar have seven days, twelve months, and 365 days, with an extra day every four years? Be aware that all the numbers in this question have certain spiritual meanings in the Scriptures. The Lord, in the creation account, not only established the calendar with its twenty-four–hour day but used it as the organization of those Scriptures. Remember the spiritual as well, as the physical are included in those creation Scriptures. The calendar, from the very beginning, has been repeated by our Lord's using it to communicate certain truths of the redemption plan of God.

The energy from the sun was created by God to sustain all physical life. God, through His Holy Spirit, gives and sustains all spiritual life. God has used the solar calendar to outline His role in His redemption plan throughout the Scriptures. The moon reflects the energy from the sun. The image of God testifies to the Lord's presence when salvation is received by faith. The Lord has used the lunar calendar to outline that which mankind receives from God. Notice as Scriptures are presented that this seems to be consistently true throughout the Scriptures.

The Seventh Day of the Calendar

From the creation account:

> And **God blessed the seventh day, and sanctified it**: because that in it he had rested from all his work which God created and made. (Genesis 2:3 KJV)

God's work was finished, and so He rested on the seventh day, which had no beginning or end. The plan for Adam's and Eve's lives, which were planned within the works of those first six days, enabled them to enter into the seventh-day rest. God's plan for the lives of everyone who will establish a faith relationship with the Lord was finished within those first six days of creation. The references to the seventh day, after the sin of Adam and Eve, are all about reestablishing that sin-cleansed relationship with the Lord, that all believers can reenter that rest.

The fourth of the Ten Commandments:

> Remember the sabbath day, to keep it holy. Six days shalt thou labour, and do all thy work: But the seventh day is the sabbath of the LORD thy God: in it thou shalt not do any work, thou, nor thy son, nor thy daughter, thy manservant, nor thy maidservant, nor

thy cattle, nor thy stranger that is within thy gates: For in six days the LORD made heaven and earth, the sea, and all that in them is, and rested the seventh day: wherefore the LORD blessed the sabbath day, and hallowed it. (Exodus 20:8–11 KJV)

The fourth of the Ten Commandments contains both the spiritual state of being available by faith to the redeemed and Saturday, the sign of the Sabbath. That is, it teaches that one cannot enter the rest of God through one's own works. First, by faith, one must be born again (justification). Then the sanctification of the Lord begins. The Lord sanctified the seventh day. Sanctification is the process of changing the redeemed to be like Christ.

Jesus said:

Come unto me, all ye that labour and are heavy laden, **and I will give you rest.** (Matthew 11:28 KJV)

No one can do anything to enter that rest except to trust Jesus to fulfill His promise that He will provide that rest. Verse 8 of the fourth commandment commands the believer to enter that spiritual rest. Verses 9 through 11 set up Saturday, the seventh day of the week, as a sign that the seventh-day spiritual rest is always available to those who would choose to live by faith. There is a separation between the sign of the seventh day of the week, Saturday, and the spiritual state being of the seventh-day rest of God, which is made clear by the following Scripture passage:

And the LORD spake unto Moses, saying, Speak thou also unto the children of Israel, saying, Verily my sabbaths ye shall keep: for it is a **sign** between me and you throughout your generations; that ye may know that I am the LORD that doth sanctify you. Ye shall keep the sabbath therefore; **for it is holy unto you**: every one that defileth it shall surely be put to death: for whosoever doeth any work therein, that soul shall be cut off from among his people. (Exodus 31:12–14 KJV)

Sabbath days—Saturdays—were the sign of God's sanctification. The Sabbath becomes holy to the redeemed through spiritual sanctification. No work on the seventh day of the week was a constant reminder each week that redemption comes only by faith and not by works.

Twelve Months in a Year

Twelve is the number that represents the witness to God's redemption plan. Remember the twelve sons of Jacob, the twelve tribes of Israel, and the twelve apostles? The meaning of the number twelve will be presented when the twelve keys of the seven notes, A to G, are played in chapter six. The twelve months of the calendar brings to mind the witness to God's redemption plan. Clocks repeat two twelve-hour periods, bringing to mind the two witnesses of God's redemption plan that began with the witness of Israel and then the witness of the church.

Three Hundred Sixty-Five Days in a Year

The 365 days of the year contain fifty-two Sabbath days. The seventh-day Sabbath-day rest of God became the experience of the redeemed on the fifty-second day after the cross. The high priest would enter the holy place of the temple on the fifty-second Sabbath day of the year, or once a year, as a sign or prophecy that redemption and the seventh-day rest would become the experience of the chosen. Israel uses the lunar calendar, so therefore it had to be aligned with the solar calendar for the high priest to know when to enter the Holy of Holies and also so the feasts could be observed at their appointed time. The instruction of the Lord to Israel was that the beginning month of months would start at the Passover. The fulfillment of that prophecy, of course, is that the solar calendar used the first advent of Christ to divide the accounting of time, using the terms BC and AD. Reconciling the solar and lunar cycles was done in three different ways: first, by observing when the new moon appeared; second, by observation and calculations; and third, by calculations only. Four of each eleven-year periods required a thirteenth month. Keep in mind that the solar and lunar cycles are not easily reconciled. The fourth year calls attention to the fourth commandment to keep the Sabbath rest holy and the fourth feast of Israel, which was Pentecost. Pentecost was when the redeemed first received the baptism of the Holy Spirit, allowing them to judicially enter the seventh-day rest by faith. The first advent of Jesus began when the fourth of the seven periods ended. The Lord established these seven periods, covering the time from the beginning of the second captivity to the final judgment, or at the end of the age. It is interesting to note that the seven periods that will end at the end of the age were also first introduced as seven days. An explanation of these seven periods will follow when we play the twelve keys in chapter six.

The Numbers Seven and Ten

The Lord used certain numbers throughout the Scriptures to help communicate spiritual truths. Two numbers are established in the creation account that are as basic to God's redemption plan as the sign of baptism and the sign of the elements of the Lord's Supper—the new birth and then sanctification by entering the Lord's seventh-day rest.

Read the Scriptures from the creation Scriptures that establish these two numbers. These are important Scriptures, as they lay the foundation for their spiritual meaning throughout the Scriptures. The ten proclamations of creation are established within the seven days in the following Scriptures from the creation account:

1. **And God said**, Let there be light: and there was light. And God saw the light, that it was good: and God divided the light from the darkness. And God called the light Day, and the darkness he called Night. And the evening and the morning were **the first day.** (Genesis 1:3–5 KJV)

2. **And God said**, Let there be a firmament in the midst of the waters, and let it divide the waters from the waters. And God made the firmament, and divided the waters which were under the firmament from the waters which were above the firmament: and it was so. And God called the firmament Heaven. And the evening and the morning were **the second day.** (Genesis 1:6–8 KJV)

3. **And God said,** Let the waters under the heaven be gathered together unto one place, and let the dry land appear: and it was so. (Genesis 1:9 KJV)

4. **And God said,** Let the earth bring forth grass, the herb yielding seed, and the fruit tree yielding fruit after his kind, whose seed is in itself, upon the earth: and it was so. ... And the evening and the morning were **the third day.** (Genesis 1:11, 13 KJV)

5. **And God said,** Let there be lights in the firmament of the heaven to divide the day from the night; and let them be for signs, and for seasons, and for days, and years: ... And the evening and the morning were **the fourth day.** (Genesis 1:14, 19 KJV)

6. **And God said,** Let the waters bring forth abundantly the moving creature that hath life, and fowl that may fly above the earth in the open firmament of heaven. ... And the evening and the morning were **the fifth day.** (Genesis 1:20, 23 KJV)

7. **And God said,** Let the earth bring forth the living creature after his kind, cattle, and creeping thing, and beast of the earth after his kind: and it was so. (Genesis 1:24 KJV)

8. **And God said,** Let us make man in our image, after our likeness: and let them have dominion

over the fish of the sea, and over the fowl of the air, and over the cattle, and over all the earth, and over every creeping thing that creepeth upon the earth. So <u>God created man in his own image, in the image of God created he him; male and female created he them</u>. And God blessed them, and God said unto them, Be fruitful, and multiply, and replenish the earth, and subdue it: and have dominion over the fish of the sea, and over the fowl of the air, and over every living thing that moveth upon the earth. (Genesis 1:26–28 KJV)

9. **And God said**, Behold, I have given you every herb bearing seed, which is upon the face of all the earth, and every tree, in the which is the fruit of a tree yielding seed; to you it shall be for meat. And to every beast of the earth, and to every fowl of the air, and to every thing that creepeth upon the earth, wherein there is life, I have given every green herb for meat: and it was so. And God saw every thing that he had made, and, behold, it was very good. And the evening and the morning were **the sixth day.** (Genesis 1:29–31 KJV). **Thus t**he heavens and the earth were finished, and all the host of them. And on the seventh day God ended his work which he had made; and he rested on the seventh day from all his work which he had made. And God blessed **the seventh day,** and **sanctified it: because that in it he had rested from all his work which God created and made.** (Genesis 2:1–3 KJV)

10. And the LORD God said, It is not good that the man should be alone; I will make him an help meet for him. (Genesis 2:18 KJV)

The ten **proclamations of creation** have been numbered. The first nine begin, "then God said," and the tenth, "then the **Lord** God said." The tenth proclamation was on the seventh day. Adam and Eve were in the image of God; that is, the indwelling Holy Spirit was with them, allowing them to enter into the seventh-day rest. God had become the Lord of their lives. The first six days have a beginning and end. The seventh has no beginning or end. The state of being of the seventh day will always exist, as God is eternal.

Ten Is the First Primary Number in God's Redemption Plan

The tenth proclamation:

Then the LORD God said, "It is not good for the man to be alone; I will make him a helper suitable for him. (Genesis 2:18)

The tenth proclamation was on the seventh day. The millions of details of the creation account are summed up in ten proclamations. Notice that access to participate in God's creation, which was completed on the sixth day, was given to Adam and Eve on the seventh day. God simply became the Lord of Adam and Eve's lives when the tenth proclamation was given. God choose the redeemed through His foreknowledge and then predestined them to be His sons through faith in Jesus Christ. This was all done within the first nine proclamations of the creation story. Yes, the freedom of mankind to choose is maintained within God's predestined redemption plan.

> Blessed be the God and Father of our Lord Jesus Christ, who hath blessed us with all spiritual blessings in heavenly places in Christ: According as he hath chosen us in him before the foundation of the world, that we should be holy and without blame before him in love: Having **predestinated us unto the adoption** of children by Jesus Christ to himself, according to the good pleasure of his will. (Ephesians 1:3–5 KJV)

Throughout the Scriptures, the number ten could be simply referring to these ten proclamations, as the redemption plan of God was worked out before the foundation of the world; that is, God's plan for every person's life who will accept Jesus by faith has been worked out from the foundation of the world. That's what makes His rest the rest of God. It has already been planned by God. The number ten is used in many ways in God's Word, but primarily it centers—after mankind was separated from the Lord—on the multiple cleansings by our Lord as he returns the lost to God the Father, to reestablish His creation as it was intended from the beginning.

Think about these examples that either point to the cleansing work of Christ or are reference to that cleansing:

The ten generations from Adam to Noah: The first overview of the gospel is presented using these ten generations.

The ten plagues: the tenth resulted in the sign of the Passover. The tenth then calls attention to the cross, which was the fulfillment of the sign of the Passover.

The Ten Commandments: these were given at Mount Sinai. The events of Mount Sinai were a type or shadow of Pentecost. This law was written on the hearts of the redeemed at Pentecost after the cleansing work of Christ.

The ten linen curtains over the tabernacle: the two barriers between man and God that formed the roof of the tabernacle were the eleven goat skins and the ten linen curtains. The first barrier, the goat skins, required a blood sacrifice. The born-again experience or the experience of baptism of the Holy Spirit requires repentance from sin, as well as faith that Jesus will cleanse those sins through His blood sacrifice. The ten linen curtains represent the continual cleansing from sin necessary for the redeemed to stay in fellowship with the Lord. Linen is referred to as the "righteous acts of the saints" in the book of Revelation. The righteousness of God becomes a reality when one continually is cleansed from sin. These ten linen curtains were created by joining two curtains, containing five curtains each, by placing fifty loops on the edge of each of the two curtains and then joining them with fifty gold clasps. The symbolism is that God's cleansing has been manifested in the two witnesses that represent the old and new covenant periods and are joined when the redeemed becomes one through the experience of Pentecost.

There were ten cleansing bowls in Solomon's temple. Each of these had a golden lamp stand with it. That is, there were ten golden lamp stands with seven lamps on each of them. Oil would flow out of the lamp stand into the seven lamps. Oil is a type of the Holy Spirit, flowing out through the lives of the redeemed when cleansed (as symbolized by the ten cleansing bowls) from ongoing sin, and then the seventh-day rest is experienced. These also were divided with five on the right and five on the left.

The diameter of the bronze sea in Solomon's temple was ten cubits. Ten times three is given as the circumference. This is not simply a dimension, as 3 x 10 does not make a circle. Ten, the multiple cleansings, were completed on cross, which resulted in the resurrection of our Lord on the third day.

How about 10 x 4 = 40, or ten, the multiple cleansings, times the end of the fourth period. Many times in Scripture, forty is the sign of the first advent of the Lord. The Lord identified with that sign by appearing forty days, starting on resurrection Sunday and ending at His ascension. Be aware that the number forty is used in many different contexts in the Scripture. The difference between a purely quantitative number and one that has had a spiritual meaning is only understood when the Lord unveils the meaning.

It was ten days from the ascension of our Lord to Pentecost—10 x 5 = 50. The fifth period of God's redemption plan ended at Pentecost, based on the internal evidence of John's writings. The new birth became the experience of the church at Pentecost.

There were ten virgins in the parable when the Lord used marriage as a sign of the relationship with the Lord that allows one to be included in God's kingdom. Oil is a type of the Holy Spirit in that parable. The number ten is focused on the redemption of the chosen through the cleansing work of Christ in these Scriptures.

Yes, the tithe has been presented in the Scriptures as "a tenth," "the tenth," and "one-tenth."

Ten, then, more specifically has been observed as entrenched in the Scriptures, referring to the multiple tasks of the cleansing work of Jesus.

Keep in mind that the spiritual meaning of these numbers surely has been unveiled or this writing simply would not have happened. The evidence that certain numbers have been used to communicate spiritual truths, of course, is in the Scriptures. As the Scriptures are read, watch that the Lord used the numbers ten and seven in different forms to communicate spiritual truths consistent with all the Scriptures.

Seven Is the Second of the Two Primary Numbers in God's Redemption Plan

The number seven in the Scriptures primarily refers to the spiritual rest of God. Sometimes it is used as a composite with another number that describes a period or completion of some phase of the redemption plan of God. An example of this is ten times seven, or seventy. The seven days of the seventieth week of Daniel became the Day of Atonement and then provided access to the seventh-day rest, until the Lord's second coming for all the chosen saved. The feast of the Day of Atonement was observed on the seventh month and the tenth day. The seven days of the seventieth week of Daniel also became a sign of the Lord's second coming. This sign was to be given by the chosen race of Israel. The first three and a half years are in the history books from AD mid-66 until AD 70 when the temple was destroyed. The last three and a half of the seven days of the seventieth week of Daniel, when completed, will result in the return of the Lord. Remember that the days become years in the seventy weeks of Daniel for the sign of Israel. Those years have been called prophetic years, as they are based on a thirty-day (10 x 3) month. The number seven is also used as a signpost pointing to the seventh-day rest.

31

Jesus Entered the Seventh Day after
the Sixth Day of the Cross

Jesus fulfilled the sign of the Sabbath, Saturday, the day after the cross. Jesus went to the cross on the sixth day to redeem the lost. Everyone from Adam's sin to the end of the age has been born into that state of the sixth day of creation, separated from God. Jesus was in the tomb or absent from a physical presence in this world on the seventh day. Jesus has been absent physically from this world from the day He ascended until He will return at His second coming. His spiritual kingdom has become the experience of the redeemed. Ever since that seventh day after the cross, He has been reigning over his kingdom and is Lord to the redeemed over the seventh day rest. Remember that Jesus said he would give this rest to whoever would come to Him. The process of sanctification begins for the chosen saved when the redeemed choose to enter His rest.

Jesus arose on the first day of the week but also on His eighth day, as he was the first of the firstfruits. That is, He was the first to experience the bodily resurrection that the redeemed will experience when the chosen saved enter the eighth day period at His second coming. Jesus had no sin of His own to keep Him in the grave.

Sunday has become the day that is set aside to acknowledge this, as Jesus was resurrected on this day. <u>The sign of the seventh-day Sabbath rest has been fulfilled</u>.

> For if Joshua had given them rest, He would not have
> spoken of another day after that. There **remains**
> <u>therefore a Sabbath rest for the people of God</u>. For

the one who has entered His rest has himself also rested from his works, as God did from His. Let **us therefore be diligent to enter that rest,** lest anyone fall through following the same example of disobedience. (Hebrews 4:8–11 NASB)

The writer of Hebrews calls attention to the separation that exists from the seventh-day rest. Because this Scripture was written after the cross, the seventh-day rest is now available, and in fact this Scripture calls to attention that we are disobedient if we don't enter that rest by faith each day of our lives.

Throughout the Scriptures, seven refers to the state of being of the seventh-day rest. Many times the number is used as a signpost to refer to that spiritual state of being. Seven days in the calendar is an example of this type of organizational signpost.

There is one body, and one Spirit, even as ye are called in one hope of your calling; One Lord, one faith, one baptism, One God and Father of all, who is above all, and through all, and in you all. But unto every one of us is given grace according to the measure of the gift of Christ. Wherefore he saith, **When he ascended up on high, he led captivity captive,** and **gave gifts unto men.** (Now that he ascended, what is it but that he also descended first into the lower parts of the earth? He that descended is the same also that ascended up far above all heavens, that he might fill all things.) (Ephesians 4:4–10 KJV)

Jesus came to earth and freed all who would accept His forgiveness from their sin. Sin is what holds mankind captive. The spiritual resurrection has become a reality with the new birth. When Jesus descended, He gave gifts to the chosen saved. Read the following Scriptures, and keep in mind that these are a continuation of Ephesians 4:8–10.

> And he gave some, apostles; and some, prophets; and some, evangelists; and some, pastors and teachers; For the perfecting of the saints, for the work of the ministry, for the edifying of the body of Christ. (Ephesians 4:11–12 KJV)

Every newborn child of God has a calling and is equipped with spiritual gifts to fulfill that calling. The fulfillment of reigning with Christ throughout the church age is accomplished when each ministry and spiritual gift is recognized. When the local church chooses to conform to the Lord's spiritual church, great things happen. People are saved. Praise the Lord.

Marriage between Man and Woman

The details of the marriage between Adam and Eve were given as part of the tenth proclamation on the seventh day. They were created at the eighth proclamation on the sixth day. The redeemed will enter the eighth period at the return of the Lord at the end of the events of the sixth trumpet or at the blowing of the seventh trumpet of the seventh seal of the book of Revelation.

These many Scriptures that focus on marriage have been included at this point for two reasons: (1) the spiritual principles of marriage find their origin within the details of the seventh-day rest. The details are in the tenth proclamation on the seventh day of creation; and (2) these principles must be fully understood, as they are involved in the unveiling of many Scriptures that will be visited in this writing, because those principles are entrenched deeply in their spiritual meaning.

> And the LORD God said, It is not good that the man should be alone; I will make him an help meet for him. ... Therefore shall a man leave his father and his mother, and shall cleave unto his wife: and **they shall be one flesh.** (Genesis 2:18; 24:18 KJV)

> The Pharisees also came unto him, tempting him, and saying unto him, Is it lawful for a man to put away his wife for every cause? And he answered and said unto them, Have ye not read, that he which made them at the beginning made them male and female, And said, For this cause shall a man leave father and mother, and shall cleave to his wife: and they twain shall be one flesh? Wherefore they are no more twain, but one flesh. **What therefore God hath joined together, let not man put asunder.** They say unto him, Why did Moses then command to give a writing of divorcement, and to put her away? He saith unto them, Moses because of the hardness of your hearts suffered you to put away your wives: **but from the beginning it was not so.** (Matthew 19:3–8 KJV)

Divorce was never in God's original plan for those who enter into the marriage relationship. Everyone has a fallen carnal nature that Adam and Eve did not have when they chose to sin and be separated from God. This fallen carnal nature makes it impossible for one to not sin, as the Scriptures have said that everything not done through faith is sin. The Lord has presented, is presenting, and will present an opportunity to every person for a faith relationship with Him. The Lord has promised that He will maintain one's relationship with Him, which is established through the new birth, throughout the church age. The redeemed are the Lord's, no matter what.

"Return, O backsliding children," says the LORD; **"for I am married to you**. I will take you, one from a city and two from a family, and I will bring you to Zion. And I will give you shepherds according to My heart, who will feed you with knowledge and understanding." (Jeremiah 3:14 NKJV)

Marriage Is a Sign of the Redeemed's Relationship with God

The kingdom of heaven is like unto a certain king, which made a marriage for his son, And sent forth his servants to call them that were bidden to the wedding: and they would not come. Again, he sent forth other servants, saying, Tell them which are bidden, Behold, I have prepared my dinner: my oxen and my fatlings are killed, and all things are ready: come unto the marriage. But they made light of it, and went their ways, one to his farm, another to his merchandise. (Matthew 22:2–5 KJV)

Then saith he to his servants, The wedding is ready, but they which were bidden were not worthy. Go ye therefore into the highways, and as many as ye shall find, bid to the marriage. (Matthew 22:8–9 KJV)

The Lord used marriage in this parable to communicate truths about His kingdom. The chosen were not responding to the call, so the invitation was sent out to all, that they might have the opportunity to respond to a faith relationship with Him.

Then shall the kingdom of heaven be likened unto ten virgins, which took their lamps, and went forth to meet the bridegroom. (Matthew 25:1 KJV)

This is yet another parable that used the sign of marriage to present truths of His kingdom. The number ten calls attention to the cleansing that was necessary to fill their lamps with oil, which was a type of the indwelling Holy Spirit within them. The result was that they were ready to enter the Lord's kingdom.

And the **third** day there **was a marriage** in Cana of Galilee; and the mother of Jesus was there: And both Jesus was called, and his disciples, to the marriage. And when they wanted wine, the mother of Jesus saith unto him, They have no wine. Jesus saith unto her, Woman, what have I to do with thee? **mine hour is not yet come**. His mother saith unto the servants, Whatsoever he saith unto you, do it. And there were set there **six** waterpots of stone, after the manner of

37

the purifying of the Jews, containing **two or three** firkins apiece. (John 2:1–6 KJV)

The six water pots call attention to the Lord's hour, which was on the sixth day. Two or three may call attention to the two witnesses and the three divisions of time of the witness. Remember these numbers appear in the context of the sign of the third day, a marriage, and the Lord's hour. Many have understood this Scripture as the spiritual marriage between God and man, as some have called their local churches the "new wine church." Equating His hour with the sixth hour of the sixth day brings this Scripture alive. The Lord began with water, a symbol of cleansing, in six pots or on the sixth day, and then on the sixth day He cleansed all the redeemed from their sins. Who are the redeemed in this Scripture? They are the ones who have chosen a faith relationship with the Lord throughout the three divisions of time of the witness to God's redemption plan, and with understanding through the two witnesses of the last two of the three divisions of time.

Understanding the parallel, or sign, of marriage to the faith relationship with God is foundational to understanding many Scriptures. It is why several Scriptures have been included at this point of this writing. The details of Adam and Eve's being joined together were on the seventh day of the creation story, while they were experiencing the seventh-day rest relationship with God. Joining this marriage sign with the sign of certain numbers will be used to discover the organization of God's two witnesses in the sixth chapter of this writing.

Chickens hatch in twenty-one days, on <u>average</u>. I know this to be true, as it happens every time we set eggs to hatch. I recently found the list below but do not know if it is accurate. Notice that all the numbers are divisible by seven. Is it possible that the Lord has engrained the sign of the seventh-day rest in these numbers?

Potato bugs hatch in seven days. Canaries hatch in fourteen days (7 x 2). Barnyard hens hatch in twenty-one days (7 x 3). Ducks and geese hatch in twenty-eight days (7 x 4). Mallards hatch thirty-five days (7 x 5). Parrots and ostriches hatch in forty-two days (7 x 6). Chapter 4 of this writing explains what happens at forty-nine days (7 x 7).

3

671-8   1   1   1   1   1   1   1

ab def gabcdef gabcdef gabcdef gabcdef ga bcdef gabcdef gabc
C

Play this C as the first and eighth days of the week.

The third key of C is played for resurrection Sunday. Sunday, resurrection day, is the first day of the week for the church. It is the eighth day for Christ, as the first of the first-fruits prophecy to receive His spiritual body. Jesus had no sin, which resulted in His bodily resurrection on **the third** day.

The re-creation of the redeemed—that is, the resurrection of the body—will be completed at the second coming of our Lord, when the literal eighth day period begins for the chosen saved.

> Also in the <u>fifteenth day</u> of the **seventh month**, when ye have **gathered in the fruit of the land**, ye shall keep a feast unto the LORD **seven** days: on the **first** day shall be a sabbath, and on the **eighth** day shall be a sabbath. (Leviticus 23:39 KJV)

This Scripture comes from the seventh of the seven feasts or the seventh of the eight appointed times given to Israel that recap the overview of God's redemption plan, as presented throughout the first captivity of Israel. The eighth appointed time was the sign, Saturday, of the seventh-day rest. Read Leviticus 23–25. This seventh feast of the booths is a prophecy of the New Testament church age. It begins with Pentecost, **"gathered in the fruit of the land,"** and continues until the return of our Lord. The seventh-day rest—**"seven** days"—is available by faith to every born-again believer, which results in a continuous worship experience with our Lord. Our Lord fulfilled the sign of the Saturday rest on the day after the cross. We then gather together on Sunday, the **"first** day" of the week, to worship our Lord. The first day then becomes a sign of the **"eighth** day" period that will have no beginning or end. The seventh-day rest will become literal throughout the time that has been referred to as the eighth-day rest.

When the Scriptures are read, the number three refers more times than not to the resurrection of our Lord on the third day. Ten, the multiple cleansings of our Lord, times three, or thirty, simply means that the Lord has completed the sacrifice for the sins of the chosen. Example: Levi was the **third** of the **eight** sons born through the two marriages of Jacob. The tribe of Levi became the priests to the chosen Israel throughout their witness. Jesus fulfilled the sign of these priests, and the priesthood of the believer became possible with His resurrection on the third day.

The Resurrection of Jesus Prophesied

Then on **the third day** Abraham lifted up his eyes, and saw the place afar off. And Abraham said unto his young men, Abide ye here with the ass; and I and the lad will go yonder and worship, and come again to you, And Abraham took the wood of the burnt offering, and laid it upon Isaac his son; and he took the fire in his hand, and a knife; and they went both of them together. And Isaac spake unto Abraham his father, and said, My father: and he said, Here am I, my son. And he said, Behold the fire and the wood: but where is the lamb for a burnt offering? And Abraham said, My son, **God will provide himself a lamb** for a burnt offering: **so they went both of them together.** (Genesis 22:4–7 KJV)

On the third day, the father and the son went forward willingly for the sacrifice. God the Father and Jesus the Son fulfilled this prophecy. Abraham was a type of the father, and Isaac was a type of the son. Later, Jacob would be presented as a type of the Holy Spirit. Abraham was the father of the chosen race of Israel, but it was Jacob whose name was changed to Israel.

And Joseph saw Ephraim's children **of the third generation**: the children also of Machir the son Manasseh were brought up upon Joseph's knees. (Genesis 50:23 KJV)

All that were **numbered of the camp of Ephraim** were an hundred thousand and eight thousand and an hundred, throughout their armies. And they shall go forward in **the third rank.** (Numbers 2:24 KJV)

The tribe of Judah was to set out first, then the tribe of Reuben, and then, **third**, the tribe of **Ephraim**. These Scriptures come alive when one understands the spiritual meaning of the number three and the role of Ephraim in the redemption plan of God. Joseph, the seventh son to the two marriages, was the type of the Christ among the twelve sons of Jacob. Joseph had two sons—whom Jacob (who became Israel) blessed before he died—who joined them into the twelve tribes of the first witness, Israel. Joseph's tribe was split between the older son, Manasseh, and the younger son, Ephraim. Manasseh represents the presence of Jesus throughout the old covenant, and Ephraim represents the work of Jesus throughout the new covenant. Joshua was from the tribe of Judea, the tribe of the lineage of Jesus, and Caleb was from the tribe of Ephraim—both tribes were represented, as they led the chosen into the Holy Land. Both of these tribes are prophecies of the Lord, leading the chosen saved into that place that has been prepared for them at His second coming. More details on this in chapter 6.

> At the end of **three years** thou shalt bring forth all the
> **tithe** of thine increase the same year, and shalt lay it
> up within thy gates. (Deuteronomy 14:28 KJV)

This Scripture was added just to stimulate the mind. After all, what does the number three have to do with the multiple-cleansing number, ten? When one is born again, the new spiritual nature wants to give, while the old carnal nature wants to receive. The Scriptures say something about its being more blessed to give.

> And the LORD said unto Moses, Go unto the people,
> and sanctify them to day and to morrow, and let them

43

wash their clothes, And be ready against the third day: **for the third day the LORD will come down in the sight of all the people** upon mount Sinai. (Exodus 19:10–11 KJV)

And it came to pass on the third day in the morning, that there were thunders and lightnings, and a thick cloud upon the mount, and the voice of the trumpet exceeding loud; so that all the people that was in the camp trembled. And **Moses brought forth the people out of the camp to meet with God;** and they stood at the nether part of the mount. (Exodus 19:16–17 KJV)

Mount Sinai was where the Lord revealed knowledge, through the Law, to the chosen Israel. When the chosen saved are raised up with Christ on the third day, that Law is written in their hearts. What happened at Sinai helped define sin but was just a signpost of knowing God though the spiritual resurrection. The indwelling Holy Spirit fulfilled the sign of Moses' bringing the people to meet God.

Come, and let us return unto the LORD: for he hath torn, and he will heal us; he hath smitten, and he will bind us up. After two days will he revive us: <u>in the third day he will raise us up</u>, and we shall live in his sight. (Hosea 6:1–2 KJV)

And he put the wood in order, and cut the bullock in pieces, and laid him on the wood, and said, Fill **four** barrels with water, and pour it on the burnt <u>sacrifice</u>, and on the wood. And he said, Do it the second time.

And they did it the second time. And he said, Do it **the third time**. And they did it the third time. And the water ran round about the altar; and he filled the trench also **with water**. And it came to pass at the time of the offering of the evening sacrifice, that Elijah the prophet came near, and said, LORD God of Abraham, Isaac, and of Israel, let it be known this day that thou art God in Israel, and that I am thy servant, and that I have done all these things at thy word. (1 Kings 18:33–36 KJV)

The spiritual meaning of the number three helps identify the sign of Elijah's sacrifice on the altar with the sacrifice of our Lord. Elijah's sacrifice was a signpost, although it did get the attention of those who witnessed it, pointing to the sacrifice of our Lord. It was not what Elijah did but what God did that got their attention. Did you notice that there were four barrels? The Lord came to the cross at the end of the fourth period. Rome was the fourth of the four kingdoms that were prophesied in the book of Daniel.

And this house was finished on **the third day** of the month Adar, which was in the **sixth year** of the reign of Darius the king. (Ezra 6:15 KJV)

The first temple of the Holy Spirit is the body of Jesus in God's redemption plan. Solomon's temple was all about the cleansing work of Christ. The second temple of the Holy Spirit is the body of the church; that is, all those who have been born again. Zerubbabel's temple was all about the cleansing of the redeemed. The spiritual meanings of these numbers bring this Scripture alive. The prophecy or sign of this second temple was fulfilled after the sacrifice of Jesus on the sixth day of the week and His resurrection on the third day.

> Speak unto the children of Israel, and say unto them, When ye be come into the land which I give unto you, and shall reap the harvest thereof, then ye shall bring a sheaf of **the firstfruits** of your harvest unto the priest: And he shall wave the sheaf before the LORD, to be accepted for you: on the morrow after the sabbath the priest shall wave it. (Leviticus 23:10–11 KJV)

This Scripture comes from the third of the seven feasts given to Israel that became foundational to the witness of Israel. These seven feasts were prophecies of the core events of God's redemption plan, starting at the cross and ending at the second coming of our Lord. Jesus, at His resurrection on the third day, was to become the first of the firstfruits to be resurrected.

> From that time forth began Jesus to shew unto his disciples, how that he must go unto Jerusalem, and suffer many things of the elders and chief priests and scribes, and be killed, and be raised again **the third day.** (Matthew 16:21 KJV)

> Saying, The Son of man must suffer many things, and be rejected of the elders and chief priests and scribes, and be slain, and be raised **the third day.** (Luke 9:22 KJV)

Jesus simply continued the prophecy that He would rise on the third day. The number three is used repeatedly throughout the Scriptures, referring to the Lord's resurrection.

The Resurrection of the Chosen Saved Prophesied

And at that time shall Michael stand up, the great prince which standeth for the children of thy people: and there shall be a time of trouble, such as never was since there was a nation even to that same time: and **at that time thy people shall be delivered**, every one that shall be found written in the book. And many of them that sleep in the dust of the earth **shall awake, some to everlasting life**, and some to shame and everlasting contempt. And they that be wise shall shine as the brightness of the firmament; and they that turn many to righteousness as the stars for ever and ever. But thou, O Daniel, shut up the words, and seal the book, even to the time of the end: many shall run to and fro, and knowledge shall be increased. (Daniel 12:1–4 KJV)

Two bodily resurrections are contained in these verses—the resurrection of the saints, and the resurrection of those destined to be separated from the Lord forever. Many Scriptures confirm that these two resurrections do not happen at the same time. The "hour is coming" indicates that they are not far apart. The saints will be resurrected to a judgment and reward for their good works at the beginning of the final tribulation on the world. The lost will be resurrected to a judgment for their sin at the end of the final tribulation period. That final tribulation period is a period of judgment on the world.

Thy dead men shall live, together with my dead body **shall they arise**. Awake and sing, ye that dwell in dust: for thy dew is as the dew of herbs, and the earth shall cast out the dead. (Isaiah 26:19 KJV)

But as touching the resurrection of the dead, have ye not read that which was spoken unto you by God, saying, I am the God of Abraham, and the God of Isaac, and the God of Jacob? God is not the God of the dead, but of the living. (Matthew 22:31–32 KJV)

Marvel not at this: for the **hour is coming**, in the which all that are in the graves shall hear his voice, And shall come forth; they that have done good, unto the resurrection of life; and they that have done evil, unto the resurrection of damnation. (John 5:28–29 KJV)

The Resurrection of Jesus on the Third Day

But now is Christ risen from the dead, and become the firstfruits of them that slept. For since by man came death, by man came also the resurrection of the dead. For as in Adam all die, even so in Christ shall all be made alive. But every man in his own order: Christ the **firstfruits**; afterward they that are Christ's at his coming. (1 Corinthians 15:20–23 KJV)

Jesus was the fulfillment of the third feast, of the first seven feasts of Israel, as the **first** of the firstfruits.

Concerning his Son Jesus Christ our Lord, which was made of the seed of David according to the flesh; And declared to be the Son of God with power, according to the spirit of holiness, by the **resurrection from the dead.** (Romans 1:3–4 KJV)

The God of our fathers raised up Jesus, whom ye slew and hanged on a tree. Him hath God exalted with his right hand to be a Prince and a Savior, for to give repentance to Israel, and forgiveness of sins. And <u>we are his witnesses</u> of these things; and <u>so is also the Holy Ghost, whom God hath given to them that obey him.</u> (Acts 5:30–32 KJV)

Prophecies of the resurrection were given over hundreds of years and then fulfilled in great detail by Jesus. Those who were with Jesus as the resurrection came to pass testified that they were witnesses to the event. Praise the Lord that above and beyond this evidence is the presence of the Holy Spirit within us, who lets us know, beyond anything else, that the resurrection is real.

And it **was the third hour,** and they crucified him. (Mark 15:25 KJV)

For I delivered unto you first of all that which I also received, how that Christ died for our sins according to the scriptures; And that he was buried, and that he rose again **the third day** according to the scriptures. (1 Corinthians 15:3–4 KJV)

The <u>Spiritual</u> Resurrection of the Chosen Saved

And ye shall count unto you **from the morrow after the sabbath**, from the day that ye brought the sheaf of the wave offering; **seven sabbaths shall be complete**: Even unto **the morrow after the seventh sabbath shall ye number fifty days**; and ye shall offer a new meat offering unto the LORD. Ye shall bring out of your habitations **two** wave loaves of **two tenth** deals: they shall be of fine flour; they shall be baken with leaven; **they are the firstfruits unto the LORD.** (Leviticus 23:15–17 KJV)

These verses from Leviticus are also from the third feast of the firstfruits. This prophecy included all the chosen saved as firstfruits of the harvest through the spiritual resurrection that is the born-again experience.

"**From the morrow after the Sabbath**": The first feast, Passover, was on the fourteenth day of the first month; the second feast, unleavened bread, was on the fifteenth day of the first month; and the third feast, firstfruits, was on the sixteenth day of the first month. The third feast was on Sunday resurrection day. This confirms that the first feast, Passover, was on Friday, the sixth day of the week.

"**Seven sabbaths shall be <u>complete</u>**": Seven Sabbaths times seven days completes the old covenant. (Chapter 4 will review this period.) The word "complete" is where this writer first became aware that the multiplication of numbers is used to show completeness in the Scriptures. Seven Sabbath days times seven days is forty-nine days.

"**The morrow after the seventh sabbath shall ye number fifty days**": Fifty days after resurrection Sunday was Pentecost. Exodus

23:16 and other Scriptures state that the firstfruits of the harvest would be at the end of the year, or at the end of fifty-two Sabbath days from the cross. Remember that the crop harvests simply point to the spiritual harvest at Pentecost. Chapter 5 reviews the harvest.

"**Two**," "**two-tenths**," and "**they are the firstfruits unto the Lord**": The number two calls attention to the two witnesses. These numbers continue and are well established as referring to the two witnesses. Watch for them when we review the witnesses to the Lord's redemption plan. Be aware that the number two appears in many Scriptures that are centered on the firstfruits. This prophecy simply points to the all the chosen saved being added as firstfruits through the spiritual resurrection. The born-again experience, or the baptism of the Holy Spirit, first became a reality to the church or all the chosen saved at Pentecost.

The fulfillment of this prophecy of firstfruits is confirmed in the following verse from James 1:18. Jesus came at Pentecost to set up His kingdom. Remember that the chosen saved passed from death to eternal life by faith in the Lord as Savior and Lord of their lives. The chosen saved became firstfruits through the spiritual resurrection.

> In the exercise of His will He brought us forth by the word of truth, so that we might be, as it were, the first fruits among His creatures. (James 1:18 NASB)

The following Scriptures speak of being raised with Christ:

> Come, and let us return unto the LORD: for he hath torn, and he will heal us; he hath smitten, and he will bind us up. <u>After two days will he revive us</u>: **in the**

third day he will raise us up, and <u>we shall live in his sight.</u> (Hosea 6:1–2 KJV)

If **ye then be risen with Christ**, seek those things which are above, where Christ sitteth on the right hand of God. Set your affection on things above, not on things on the earth. For ye are dead, and your life is hid with Christ in God. When Christ, who is our life, shall appear, then shall ye also appear with him in glory. (Colossians 3:1–4 KJV)

Blessed be the God and Father of our Lord Jesus Christ, who according to His great mercy has caused us to **be born again to a living hope through the resurrection of Jesus Christ** from the dead, to obtain an inheritance which is imperishable and undefiled and will not fade away, reserved in heaven for you. (1 Peter 1:3–4 NASB)

In Revelation, John refers to the spiritual resurrection as the first resurrection. The second death will have no power over those who have been born again. The priesthood of the believer became a reality at Pentecost, and the church began to reign with Him. In Revelation 20, John recounts what had happened to those of the chosen saved after the tribulation began at Pentecost, as a result of their choosing to receive the first spiritual resurrection and then reign with the Lord. This chapter is about those who have been born again, reigning with our Lord throughout the church dispensation of time. They will reign until the cleansing work of Jesus is finished, as 10 x 10 x 10 is a finished number.

But the rest of the dead lived not again until the thousand years were finished. **This is the first resurrection.** Blessed and holy is **he that hath part in the first resurrection: on such the second death hath no power,** but they **shall be priests of God** and of Christ, and shall reign with him a thousand years. (Revelation 20:5–6 KJV)

The Resurrection of the Body

For the Lord Himself will descend from heaven **with a shout,** with the voice of the archangel, and with the trumpet of God; **and the dead in Christ shall rise first. Then we who are alive and remain shall be caught up together with them in the clouds to meet the Lord in the air,** and thus we shall always be with the Lord. (1 Thessalonians 4:16–17 NASB)

Whosoever shall seek to save his life shall lose it; and whosoever shall lose his life shall preserve it. I tell you, in that night there shall be two men in one bed; the one shall be taken, and the other shall be left. Two women shall be grinding together; the one shall be taken, and the other left. **Two men shall be in the field; the one shall be taken, and the other left.** And they answered and said unto him, Where, Lord? And he said unto them, Wheresoever the body is, thither will the eagles be gathered together. (Luke 17:33–37 KJV)

God finished His work of creation on the sixth day, and then there was a seventh day of rest. Jesus finished His work on the sixth day, and then there was again a seventh-day rest. When the events of the sixth trumpet are finished, then that seventh trumpet will sound, and then the events of the second coming of our Lord will be finished. The finished number of the chosen saved will be complete. The opportunity to receive the Lord as one's personnel Savior and Lord will be gone for eternity. *Do you know the Lord?* Jesus loves you, and that love sent Him to the cross for us. The time is now to respond to His precious invitation to love Him as He loves you.

> For our citizenship is in heaven, from which also we eagerly wait for a Savior, the Lord Jesus Christ; who will transform the body of our humble **state into conformity with the body of His glory**, by the exertion of the power that He has even to subject all things to Himself. (Philippians 3:20 NASB)

> It is sown a natural body; **it is raised a spiritual body**. There is a natural body, and there is a spiritual body. (1 Corinthians 15:44 KJV)

The redeemed will receive a new spiritual body like the spiritual body of Christ at His coming. The Scriptures say that we will be changed. This simply will be the Lord fulfilling His promise to all who trust Him in all things. Praise the Lord that He loves us that much that He has done and will do these things. Then comes the judgment of the works that have been done with our Lord for all the redeemed.

"But when you give a reception, invite the poor, the crippled, the lame, the blind, and you will be blessed, since they do not have the means to repay you; for you will be repaid **at the resurrection of the righteous.**" (Luke 14:13–14 NASB)

Play C to B = 49 keys.

Seven Sabbath days x seven = forty-nine days, or seven weeks.

Remember the key of B was played on Saturday, the Sabbath.

It will be interesting to learn all the reasons why the Lord chose to pay the penalty for sin on the cross and then have a period of fifty-two days before Pentecost when the cleansing from sin became judicially the experience of the chosen saved. We do know that the fifty-two days are the same as the fifty-two Sabbath days in a year. We do know that the sign of the seventh-day rest is Saturday. Remember that the goal of the redemption plan is to save precious people so they can enter God's rest. Keep in mind these two Scriptures before the year of Jubilee is reviewed.

Remember the sabbath day, to keep it holy. (Exodus 20:8 KJV)

The fourth commandment makes it quite clear that the spiritual state of being of the seventh-day rest is to be kept holy.

> And the LORD spake unto Moses, saying, Speak thou also unto the children of Israel, saying, Verily my sabbaths ye shall keep: **for it is a sign** between me and you throughout your generations; **that ye may know that I am the LORD that doth sanctify you.** Ye shall keep the sabbath therefore; for it is holy unto you: every one that defileth it shall surely be put to death: for whosoever doeth any work therein, that soul shall be cut off from among his people. (Exodus 31:12–14 KJV)

Moses revisited the instructions that accompanied the fourth commandment about Saturday, the seventh day of the week. It was made clear that Saturday is a sign of the spiritual rest of God, a sign that entering that rest results in God's sanctification process of the believer. Saturday comes once a week, reminding the chosen of God's involvement in their lives. The Holy Spirit seems to have to constantly remind us now. Joseph interpreted the dream of the cupbearer, and then declared that he would live. The Scripture says the cupbearer forgot to mention it. Jesus gave us the Lord's Supper to remind us daily of the Lord's presence in our lives, yet we still tend to forget that He has given us life. Please, Lord, forgive us of our sin.

Forty-Nine Years, Then the Year of Jubilee

> And thou shalt number <u>seven sabbaths</u> of years unto thee, **seven times seven years; and the space of the**

seven sabbaths of years shall be unto thee forty and nine years. Then shalt thou cause the trumpet of the jubile to sound on the **tenth day of the seventh month**, in the day of atonement shall ye make the trumpet sound throughout all your land. And ye shall hallow the fiftieth year, and **proclaim liberty throughout all the land** unto all the inhabitants thereof: it shall be a jubile unto you; and ye shall return every man unto his possession, and ye shall return every man unto his family. A jubile shall that fiftieth year be unto you: ye shall not sow, neither reap that which groweth of itself in it, nor gather the grapes in it of thy vine undressed. For it is the jubile; it shall be holy unto you: ye shall eat the increase thereof out of the field. In the year of this jubile ye shall return every man unto his possession. (Leviticus 25:8–13 KJV)

"**seven times seven years; and the space of the seven sabbaths of years shall be unto thee forty and nine years**": This same sign of the seven Sabbaths times seven was used in the feast of the firstfruits, pointing to the lives of the redeemed being filled with the fruit of the Spirit at Pentecost. The year of jubilee points to the fiftieth day as the time that all the chosen saved were returned to God the Father.

When two numbers are multiplied in the Scriptures, it consistently points to completion. The sign of the period of the Sabbath rest, Saturday, has been completed. It's time to enter the spiritual seventh-day rest. Be aware that Israel used forty-nine years to reconcile the solar cycle with the lunar cycle, as the error was only thirty-two hours off every forty-nine solar years. Astronomy also recognizes forty-nine solar years as a period of restitution between the solar and lunar cycles.

Keep in mind that Moses gave the instructions for the Jubilee year at Mount Sinai, which was of itself a type of the results of Pentecost. The year of Jubilee, then, was simply a physical sign of the spiritual event called Pentecost.

Seven Sabbaths times seven simply completed the old covenant, and then the next day, Pentecost began the experience of the new covenant for the chosen saved.

"tenth day of the seventh month": The sixth feast of Israel was to be held on the tenth day of the seventh month. The Day of Atonement was at Pentecost. The trumpet of the Day of Atonement was blown on the fiftieth year of Jubilee, which identifies the year of Jubilee with Pentecost. Every soul that has and will come to Jesus was judicially accounted for at Pentecost. The souls of the chosen saved were returned to the Father. Ten, the multiple cleansing of the Lord, resulted in the spiritual seventh-day rest becoming the experience of the chosen saved at Pentecost.

"proclaim liberty throughout all the land": Those in captivity of sin who love the Lord were set free at Pentecost. The instruction to Israel was to tell everyone about it. The Lord asked His church to tell everyone about this new freedom in Christ.

Forty Plus Ten Days to Pentecost

The period from resurrection Sunday to Pentecost was then divided by forty-nine days and then one day, Pentecost. This period also was divided in another way. Jesus appeared for forty days.

> To whom also he shewed himself alive after his
> passion by many infallible proofs, **being seen of them**
> **forty days**, and speaking of the things pertaining to
> the kingdom of God: And, being assembled together
> with them, commanded them that they should not
> depart from Jerusalem, but wait for the promise of
> the Father, which, saith he, ye have heard of me. (Acts
> 1:3–4 KJV)

Ten, the multiple cleansing tasks of Jesus, times four completed the fourth of the seven periods that will end with the second coming of our Lord. Jesus identified with the forty-day prophecy by fulfilling the prophecy, appearing for forty days after the resurrection. Then there were ten days to Pentecost when that multiple cleansing would be experienced by the chosen saved. Ten once again marks the multiple tasks of the cleansing of our Lord Jesus Christ that became the experience of the saved at Pentecost.

5

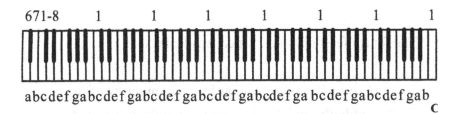

671-8   1   1   1   1   1   1   1

abcdef gabcdef gabcdef gabcdef gabcdef ga bcdef gabcdef gab
C

Play this C as the fiftieth day of Pentecost.

Fifty-two keys played—the cross to Pentecost.

The key of C was first played on Sunday, the first day of the week, or on the day of the resurrection of Jesus, and ended fifty days later on the first day of the week. A calendar year beginning on the first day of the year will also end on the first day of the week. Fifty-two weeks times seven days is 364 days. Add one day to end up with 365 days. Every fourth year, a day has to be added to the fifty-two weeks. Start with the calendar year on the first day of the week and end on the first day of the week. The second year starts on the second day and so on, from year to year, adding an extra day every fourth year. The first day of the week keeps changing for twenty-eight years, and then the cycle starts over. Within those twenty-eight years, there are three years that start on the seventh day and end on the seventh day. Those three years have an extra Sabbath day. Jesus came and fulfilled the sign of the Sabbath rest within three days from the cross to His resurrection. The calendar has been used to organize certain Scriptures, but keep in mind that the Scriptures are inspired by God.

> What? know ye not that your <u>body is the temple of the Holy Ghost</u> which is in you, which ye have of God, **and ye are not your own?** (1 Corinthians 6:19 KJV)

The fourth feast of Israel, which was Pentecost:

> And ye shall count unto you from the **morrow after the sabbath,** from the day that ye brought the sheaf of the wave offering; seven sabbaths shall be complete: Even unto the morrow after the seventh sabbath shall ye number **fifty days**; and ye shall offer a new meat offering unto the LORD. Ye shall bring out of your habitations two wave loaves of two tenth deals: they shall be of fine flour; they shall be baken with leaven; **they are the firstfruits unto the LORD.** (Leviticus 23:15–17 KJV)

All the chosen saved were returned to the God the Father judicially at Pentecost. The following is a review of some of the things that became a reality for the redeemed at Pentecost:

The Born-Again Experience

Listen as you read the words of Jesus:

> Marvel not that I said unto thee, **Ye must be born again**. The wind bloweth where it listeth, and thou

hearest the sound thereof, but canst not tell whence it cometh, and whither it goeth: so is every one that **is born of the Spirit.** (John 3:7 KJV)

The Holy Spirit can now indwell man's spirit for the first time since Adam and Eve. The spiritual birth first became the experience of the church at Pentecost. This is the baptism of the Holy Spirit. The infilling of the Holy Spirit is the ongoing experience of the work of the Holy Spirit through the lives of all who make Jesus the Lord of their lives daily. What does one do when the Holy Spirit brings conviction of the sin in one's life? Simply chose to turn from that sin and ask the Lord to forgive that sin; Scriptures promise that He will forgive. The Lord will then respond with the miracle of the new spiritual birth upon inviting Him to be one's Savior and Lord.

The Chosen Saved Regained Access to God's Righteousness

And now, little children, abide in him; that, when he shall appear, we may have confidence, and not be ashamed before him at his coming. If ye know that **he is righteous,** ye know that every **one that doeth righteousness is born of him.** (1 John 2:28–29 KJV)

And be found in him, not having mine own righteousness, which is of the law, but that which is through the faith of Christ, **the righteousness which is of God by faith.** (Philippians 3:9 KJV)

The righteousness of God is now manifested through those who are born again with the spiritual birth. Jesus said that He came to fulfill all righteousness. He will do just that through every born-again believer if we simply trust Him in all things.

God's Provision Restores

Therefore take no thought, saying, What shall we eat? or, What shall we drink? or, Wherewithal shall we be clothed? (For after all these things do the Gentiles seek:) for your heavenly Father knoweth that ye have need of all these things. But seek ye first the kingdom of God, and his righteousness; **and all these things shall be added unto you.** (Matthew 6:31–33 KJV)

By faith, God will provide all our needs. Give and serve others, and the Lord will bless. When one gives, it is out of the provision that God has already provided and will continue to provide if He is allowed by faith to do so. Praise the Lord.

Access to the Seventh-Day Rest Made Possible by the Baptism of the Holy Spirit

For if Joshua had given them rest, He would not have spoken of another day after that. There remains therefore a Sabbath rest for the people of God. **For the one who has entered His rest has himself also rested from his works,** as God did from His. Let us therefore **be diligent to enter that rest,** lest anyone fall through following the same example of disobedience. (Hebrews 4:8–11 NASB)

Jesus said that if you come to Him, He will give you rest. God rested from His works when they were done on the seventh day of creation. His works are already done. The outcome of those works has already been determined. The abundant life is all about entering God's rest, as there is freedom in His rest from all the cares of this world. God has a plan for each life, and it's already worked out. God has already worked out a solution for all the trouble that will be encountered today, tomorrow, and the next day. The state of being of the seventh-day rest is the goal of the cleansing work of our Lord. Every time the number seven appears in the Scriptures, it communicates in some manner God's rest. Remember that God's rest is by faith until the Lord returns, at which time that rest will become literal. The Scriptures have made it clear that if we fail to enter by faith, the Sabbath rest results in an act of disobedience by those who have been saved.

The Chosen Saved Are to Reign with Christ, as Access to His Kingdom Has Been Restored

And when he was demanded of the Pharisees, when the kingdom of God should come, he answered them and said, The kingdom of God cometh not with observation: Neither shall they say, Lo here! or, lo there! for, **behold, the kingdom of God is within you.** (Luke 17:20–21 KJV)

The world is constantly looking for a perfect earthly kingdom that they can see. The physical kingdoms of this earth did not come first. The spiritual kingdom of our Lord has always been and always will be. God controls this earth, although this world does not understand that. The chosen saved are to reign (sometimes translated as "serve") with Christ in His kingdom, which will triumph over the kingdoms of this earth. The Lord continually transforms the mind, which results in understanding His kingdom. Think of how much better it is when the church conforms to the organization of God's kingdom. The church will reign with Christ in His spiritual kingdom for eternity, so why not start now? Remember that an earthly king was not God's will for Israel. Have you ever heard of a church that entered into revival that the Lord did not use to win the precious lost souls?

> "Worthy are You to take the book and to break its seals; for You were slain, and purchased for God with Your blood men from every tribe and tongue and people and nation. You have made them **to be a kingdom** and **priests to our God**; and they **will reign** upon the earth." (Revelation 5:9–10 NASB)

The redeemed were first purchased by the blood of Jesus, then filled with His Holy Spirit at Pentecost, and then joined into the kingdom. The chosen no longer need to go through a priest to access the presence of God, as the priesthood of the believer has become the experience of the chosen saved. Every born-again believer has a calling that creates a place of service in the kingdom.

Communication with God Restored through God's Precious Indwelling Holy Spirit

> The voice of the LORD is upon the waters: the God of glory thundereth: the LORD is upon many waters. The voice of the LORD is powerful; the voice of the

LORD is full of majesty. The voice of the LORD breaketh the cedars; yea, the LORD breaketh the cedars of Lebanon. (Psalm 29:3–5 KJV)

The voice of the LORD divideth the flames of fire. The voice of the LORD shaketh the wilderness; the LORD shaketh the wilderness of Kadesh. The voice of the LORD maketh the hinds to calve, and discovereth the forests: and in his temple doth every one speak of his glory. (Psalm 29:7–9 KJV)

For he spake, and it was done; he commanded, and it stood fast. (Psalm 33:9 KJV)

The psalmist said that when God speaks, all these things happen. The psalmist stood in awe as he realized all the Lord had done and that it happened simply because God spoke these things into being. The world separated from God simply does not understand. Keep in mind that the Scriptures were written by man in a language of this world. Those languages came from the languages that resulted from God's confusing the original language. The writers were inspired as they wrote by God's Holy Spirit, which set these writings apart as Scriptures. The spiritual dimension that exists in the Scriptures originated from the voice of God, communicated through that original language. The Holy Spirit unveils that spiritual dimension as the redeemed read the Scriptures. The Bible becomes literal only when the voice of the Lord is heard. Remember, He is God, and we are not. The good news, of course, is that God wants every born-again believer to come to Him through His Word, that the transformation process can change us to be like Jesus.

Remember as the following Scriptures are read that this is all about language or the medium of communication between man and God—it is simply the medium through which all good things are communicated. What is communicated is what is important. Example: the fruit of the Spirit was communicated to the spirit of this writer. How? I don't know, but praise the Lord that it happened.

And when the day of Pentecost was fully come, they were all with one accord in one place. And suddenly there came a sound from heaven as of a rushing mighty wind, and it filled all the house where they were sitting. And there appeared unto them cloven tongues like as of fire, and it sat upon each of them. **And they were all filled with the Holy Ghost**, and began to speak with other tongues, **as the Spirit gave them utterance**. And there were dwelling at Jerusalem Jews, devout men, out of every nation under heaven. Now when this was noised abroad, the multitude came together, and were confounded, because that every man heard them speak in his own language. And they were all amazed and marvelled, saying one to another, Behold, are not all these which speak Galilaeans? **And how hear we every man in our own tongue, wherein we were born**? (Acts 2:1–8 KJV)

God spoke, and they all heard. God manifested His voice audibly, and all who had been baptized with the Holy Spirit and given the gift to understand heard in their own languages. Two gifts of the Holy Spirit were manifested: (1) the gift to speak in the original language was given; and (2) the gift to hear was given to understand in their language. The same thing happened that happens every day by all born-again believers when they pray. The believers pray in their own languages, and God hears them all at one time. God speaks to them, and they hear in their own languages. What happened at Pentecost was an audible sign that the indwelling Holy Spirit had reestablished communication between the spirit of man and the Spirit of God. The priesthood of the believer has come to pass. Yes, communication between God and man gave us the Scriptures, before as well as after Pentecost, but Jesus changed the prayer life of the believer when He paid the penalty for sin on the cross.

Be aware of the promise of the work of the Holy Spirit for the prayers of the believer in the following Scripture:

> How that he was caught up into paradise, **and heard unspeakable words**, which it is not lawful for a man to utter. (2 Corinthians 12:4 KJV)

That original language is a perfect language, and the prayers of the saints must be made perfect to enter into the presence of God. The Holy Spirit does just that:

> Likewise the Spirit also helpeth our infirmities: for we know not what we should pray for as we ought: but the Spirit itself maketh **intercession for us with groanings** which cannot be uttered. And he that searcheth the hearts knoweth what is the mind of the Spirit, because he maketh intercession for the saints **according to the will of God.** (Romans 8:26–27 KJV)

The Holy Spirit will only intercede in prayer when the prayer is in the will of God. The closer one walks with God, the more one's prayers are aligned with God's will.

> Follow after charity, and desire spiritual gifts, but rather that ye may prophesy. For speaketh in an unknown tongue speaketh not unto men, but unto God: for no man understandeth him; howbeit in the spirit he speaketh mysteries. But he that prophesieth speaketh unto men to edification, and exhortation, and comfort. He that speaketh in an unknown tongue edifieth himself; but he that prophesieth edifieth the church. (1 Corinthians 14:1–4 KJV)

The gift of speaking in tongues was and is a sign to Israel that Jesus was the Christ and that communication with God is now reestablished for every believer. Communication with the Lord will result in edification of the believer, whether it is done with the gift of audible speech or without it. The Scriptures make it clear that it is the redemption message that the world needs to hear. Gifts of the Holy Spirit are evidence of the baptism of the Holy Spirit, as all spiritual gifts are given when the born-again experience is manifested.

And again the Scriptures say:

> Now we have received, not the spirit of the world, but the Spirit who is from God, that we might know the things freely given to us by God, which things we also speak, *not in words taught by human wisdom,* **but in those taught by the Spirit, combining spiritual thoughts with spiritual words.** But **a natural man**

does not accept the things of the Spirit of God; for they <u>are foolishness to him, and he cannot understand them,</u> because they are spiritually appraised. (1 Corinthians 2:12–14 NASB)

The writer of Corinthians explained that the saved have a new spiritual nature as well as retaining the old carnal fallen nature. A natural man may refer to the carnal nature of the lost or the carnal nature of the believer. Being continually cleansed from sin allows the Holy Spirit to unveil the spiritual thoughts of the Lord through our new spiritual nature.

Having therefore such a hope, we use great boldness in our speech, and are not as Moses, who used to put a veil over his face that the sons of Israel might not look intently at the end of what was fading away. But their minds were hardened; for until this very day at the reading of the old covenant **the same veil remains unlifted, because it is removed in Christ**. But to this day whenever Moses is read, a veil lies over their heart; **but whenever a man turns to the Lord, the veil is taken away.** Now the Lord is the Spirit; and where the Spirit of the Lord is, there is liberty. <u>But we all, with unveiled face beholding as in a mirror the glory of the Lord, are being transformed into the same image from glory to glory, just as from the Lord, the Spirit.</u> (2 Corinthians 3:12–18 NASB)

The crossing of the Red Sea was a type of Pentecost. What happened at Mount Sinai was a type of the results of Pentecost. Yes, the Law was given on Mount Sinai, but then Jesus wrote that Law on the hearts of every believer at Pentecost. Moses's face reflected the very image of God when he came off the mountain. Jesus placed the very image of God in the faces of every believer at Pentecost. Spiritual things are unveiled in Christ.

> And even if our gospel is veiled, **it is veiled to those who are perishing**, in whose case the god of this world has blinded the minds of the unbelieving, that they might not see the light of the gospel of the glory of Christ, who is the image of God. (2 Corinthians 4:3–4 NASB)

The Bible is God's Word. The good news is that Jesus can unveil the spiritual truths and make them part of our lives if we just learn to trust Him in all things. The new spiritual nature of man can hear these truths, while the old carnal nature can't. Submit daily, and He will unveil all the spiritual truths that one needs to accomplish His will for the ministry that one is called to do on that day.

> I am the vine, ye are the branches: **He that abideth in me, and I in him, the same bringeth forth much fruit**: for without me ye can do nothing. (John 15:5 KJV)

> I can do all things through Christ which strengtheneth me. (Philippians 4:13 KJV)

Bottom line: look to the Lord continually as you read the Scriptures, as He and He alone can unveil the spiritual meanings of the Word. Using a literal translation is important. The Scriptures in this writing are from the King James Version of the Bible and the New American Standard Bible. The King James Version (KJV) does not change the numbers from the original text. This is the primary reason why it is used in this writing more than the New American Standard Bible (NASB). Certain numbers cannot be changed from the original text without changing the meaning attached to them by the Lord. The New American Standard does change or convert some numbers to present-day quantitative use. Remember that some numbers can be quantitative as well as containing a spiritual meaning. Some numbers reflect quantity only, and some numbers were never intended to reflect a quantity or dimension in the Scriptures.

God's Promise to Maintain Marriage between Man and Woman Restored

The Pharisees also came unto him, tempting him, and saying unto him, Is it lawful for a man to put away his wife for every cause? And he answered and said unto them, Have ye not read, that he which made them at the beginning made them male and female, And said, For this cause shall a man leave father and mother, and shall cleave to his wife: and they twain **shall be one flesh**? Wherefore they are no more twain, but one flesh. **What therefore God hath joined** together, **let not man put asunder.** (Matthew 19:3–6 KJV)

God's Holy Spirit and man's spirit become one when the baptism of the Holy Spirit comes upon the believer. That relationship is then secured by the work of the Holy Spirit. Notice that the same promise is given to the marriage of man and woman as they become one. Sin separated man from God, and then divorce entered into the experience of marriage between a man and woman. The penalty for sin has been paid. Two born-again believers can reclaim the promise that the Holy Spirit will maintain their marriage relationship if He is allowed to do so. Divorce should be no more. The church must hold up the spiritual principles of these two relationships if the marriage relationship is to be a witness to the redemption relationship with God. Notice how deeply these two relationships are joined within the Scriptures when there is a marriage supper of the Lamb. Christians only should be joined together in the church to keep the witness consistent with the scriptures. Can you say "Praise the Lord" with me?

We must forgive each other if the Lord is to forgive us. Remember the words of our Lord:

> For if ye forgive men their trespasses, your heavenly
> Father will also forgive you. (Matthew 6:14 KJV)

6

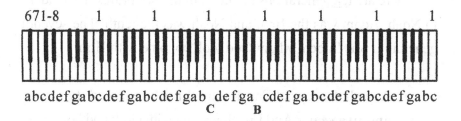

671-8   1   1   1   1   1   1   1

abcdefgabcdefgabcdefgab defga cdefga bcdefgabcdefgabc

Play all twelve keys from C to B as God's witnesses.

Seven notes yet twelve separate sounds are heard when playing these twelve keys.

The Lord has literally entrenched His redemption plan in the history of mankind because of the communication problem caused by sin. Keep in mind that the gospel is communicated much differently before the baptism of the Holy Spirit at Pentecost than after that event. Remember that the focus of the entire Bible is centered on God's redemption plan. God's plan encompasses all the choices of mankind. Experiencing God's will is the result of those choices that are made by faith in the Lord. The Lord, through the Scriptures, continually unveils spiritual truths to the believer that result in gaining certain knowledge of God's will for that person. Most of the time, God's will is simply unveiled and experienced when walking by faith. Everyone born again has a certain calling that God will unveil and then is understood. It is important to understand something of the differences between God's plan, God's will, and God's calling when reviewing the witness to His redemption plan.

The Witness to God's Redemption Plan from Adam to Noah

There are <u>ten</u> generations recorded in the Scriptures from Adam to Noah. Adam was the first, and Noah was the tenth. The <u>seventh</u> generation was Enoch, whom God took up to be with Him.

> And all the days of Enoch were **three hundred sixty and five years**: And Enoch walked with God: and he was not; **for God took him.** (Genesis 5:23–24 KJV)

Remember that ten became centered on the cleansing work of redemption so that the redeemed can enter the seventh-day rest. The phrase "for God took him" is the seventieth time that "God" appears in the Scriptures, from the beginning of the book of Genesis to this point in the fifth chapter. Ten times seven is seventy. Enoch was taken up at the beginning of the complete number seventy. Jesus went to the cross on the sixth day, which made it possible to enter the seventh day fulfilling the sign of the seven days of the seventieth week of Daniel for the redeemed. Then, on the third day, Jesus became the firstfruits of the resurrection—the experience of the first resurrection; that is, the spiritual resurrection followed at Pentecost or at the beginning of the seventieth week of Daniel for the redeemed. The seventh-day rest will become the eighth-day rest at the end of the seventieth week of Daniel for the redeemed. The sign of the seven days of week, seventy for Israel, when completed will result in the bodily resurrection of the chosen saved. The final three and a half days (years) is yet to be completed.

"three hundred sixty-five years" contain the fifty-two Sabbath days—fifty-two days from the cross to Pentecost. Enoch's faith, like all who were justified by faith prior to Pentecost, was included in the judicial accounting of the chosen saved at that time. The indwelling Holy Spirit became the experience of all the chosen saved at Pentecost. An understanding of numbers surely helps unveil the gospel in the Scriptures.

The ten generations end with Noah and the flood, which became a type of the judgment on the world that will come after the chosen saved are taken up to be with the Lord. Only eight people were ready. Eight became a sign of the fulfillment of the sign of the eighth-day Sabbath rest. When the chosen saved are taken up, they will enter the eighth-day period.

Notice the progression of the information revealed about God's plan of redemption: (1) the details of marriage were given as the tenth proclamation on the seventh day in the creation account. The tenth times seven ends with marriage, which is a type of the faith relationship with God. (2) Enoch, the seventh of ten generations, was taken up at the beginning of the seventieth. Jesus was the first to be resurrected at the beginning of the seventieth week of Daniel, which reestablished judicial access by faith to the seventh-day rest. Remember, eight people were onboard the ark. (3) Noah. the tenth generation, was taken up by the ark as judgment came to all who weren't on the boat. Noah and family were taken up at the end of the seventieth. Jesus will return for the bodily resurrection of the chosen saved when the last three and one-half days of the sign of Israel completes the seventieth week of Daniel. The church will enter the eighth-day period, and then the judgment will come on the world.

On the third day, Jesus was the first of the firstfruits to receive the bodily resurrection. All those who joined into the first resurrection of Christ by faith have received the new birth, which is the first spiritual resurrection. The bodily resurrection of Jesus was at the beginning of the seventieth week of Daniel; the bodily resurrection of the saints will be at the end of the seventieth week of Daniel when the last three and a half days are completed.

The Witness to God's Redemption Plan from Noah to Abraham

Noah was the <u>tenth</u> generation. Noah's generation ended the period of life that began with Adam and then began a new generation on and after the boat ride. The flood began as a sign of the end times. The focus of the experience on the ark then became centered on God's redemption plan, to prepare others to be ready when this prophecy would be fulfilled. God gave Noah instructions before the flood as to how to build the boat and the provisions for it. Then it rained. God has given instructions and made the provisions for salvation, so one can be ready for the second coming of Jesus.

> In the six hundredth year of Noah's life, in **the second month, the seventeenth day** of the month, the same day were all the fountains of the great deep broken up, and the windows of heaven were opened. And the rain was upon the earth **forty days** and forty nights. (Genesis 7:11–12 KJV)

> And the waters prevailed upon the earth an **hundred and fifty days.** (Genesis 7:24 KJV)

Remember that the Lord identified with the "**forty days**," as he appeared forty days with the disciples from His resurrection to His ascension. Ten times four completes the fourth of the seven periods in the timeline that the Lord organized to provide information as to the first and second advents of our Lord. The fourth period ended at the birth of Jesus. The fifth of the seven feasts was the blowing of the trumpets that was fulfilled when the angels announced the birth of Christ. God's instruction to Israel was that this feast be held on the first day of the <u>seventh month</u>. The ark came to rest in the <u>seventh month</u>. The ark began its journey in the second month and ended its journey in the seventh month. Ten, the sign of the multiple cleansing works of Jesus, times the five months is fifty. The ark resting on the mountain became a sign of Pentecost, as well as a sign of the end of the fifth of the seven periods of time that were prophesied through the generation of Joshua and then again through Daniel.

> And the ark rested **in the seventh month, on the seventeenth day of the month**, upon the mountains of Ararat. And the waters decreased continually until **the tenth month**: in the tenth month, on the first day of the month, were the tops of the mountains seen. (Genesis 8:4–5 KJV)

The sign of the seventh and the tenth are used as they were in the first ten generations from Adam to Noah. Then the Lord did something to find out when the boat ride would be over, which only can be understood when grounded in the knowledge of the seventh-day rest.

> Also he sent forth a dove from him, to see if the waters were abated from off the face of the ground;

But the dove found no rest for the sole of her foot, and she returned unto him into the ark, for the waters were on the face of the whole earth: then he put forth his hand, and took her, and pulled her in unto him into the ark. And he stayed yet other **seven days**; and again he sent forth the dove out of the ark; And the dove came in to him in the evening; and, lo, in her mouth was an olive leaf pluckt off: so **Noah knew** that the waters were abated from off the earth. And he stayed yet other **seven days**; and sent forth the dove; which returned not again unto him any more. (Genesis 8:8–12 KJV)

A raven was sent out first, before Noah sent out a dove. The raven didn't return. The raven probably was a sign of the need for redemption in this world. The raven was designated as an unclean bird in the book of Deuteronomy. Sending out the dove is the first organizational information of the three periods of the witness to God's redemption plan.

Noah sent out the dove, a type of the Holy Spirit, after the first period of God's redemption plan, and it came back with nowhere to rest. The second period begins after the sign of the first seven; that is, the first seven days in Genesis 8:10. The dove came back with an olive leaf. Noah received knowledge from this period. The third period begins after the sign of the second seven; that is, the seven days in verse 12. The dove did not return. Notice that there are only two sevens. There are three sevens with each following a six, but the third seven occurs after the chosen saved have been resurrected at the second coming of Jesus. The third six is the end of the sixth trumpet of the seventh seal of Revelation.

Identifying these three periods will be confirmed by combining what is in this Scripture with later information given within the marriages of Jacob. This will be done when the witness of Israel is introduced.

The first period is from Adam to Abraham. The Holy Spirit could not indwell the chosen saved during this period. The Holy Spirit did encamp with those who trusted Him in all things. The dove, as a type of the Holy Spirit, could find no one without sin. The second period began after the first of three sevens. This period was from Abraham to the first advent of our Lord. Knowledge came to Noah throughout this period. Knowledge of God's redemption plan was expanded, as man continued to move away from God. The entire Old Testament was written during this period. The dove still had to return, though, as it could not find a place to land. The Holy Spirit did encamp with the chosen saved but still could not find anyone cleansed from sin. The third period began after the second seven. This period of time was from the first advent of Jesus until His second advent. The dove did not come back this time, as the Holy Spirit found precious souls that had been cleansed from their sin. The dove found a resting place by indwelling the lives of all the chosen saved.

Be aware that the second seven is often referred to as fourteen in the Scripture. Example: the genealogy of Jesus, given in the book of Matthew, is divided into three groups of fourteen. Fourteen is the two sevens. A number repeated three times simply means that it is finished. Remember that God said at the end of the creation account that it was <u>finished</u>. Jesus said on the cross that it was <u>finished</u>. God will say at Jesus's second coming that it is <u>finished</u>. Jesus came at the second seven (fourteen) to fulfill this prophecy.

And it came to pass in the six hundredth and first year, in the first month, the first day of the month, the waters were dried up from off the earth: and Noah removed the covering of the ark, and looked, and, behold, the face of the ground was dry. **And in the second month, on the seven and twentieth day of the month**, was the earth dried. And God spake unto Noah, saying, Go forth of the ark, thou, and thy wife, and thy sons, and thy sons' wives with thee. (Genesis 8:13–16 KJV)

The boat ride ended in the second month on the twenty-seventh day. It began in the second month on the seventeenth day, per Genesis 7:11. That is one year—fifty-two Sabbath days plus ten days. Ten, the multicleansing from sin, became the experience of the chosen saved at Pentecost.

And Noah builded an altar unto the LORD; and took of every clean beast, and of every clean fowl, and offered burnt offerings on the altar. And the LORD smelled a sweet savour; and the LORD said in his heart, I will not again curse the ground any more for man's sake; for the imagination of man's heart is evil from his youth; neither will I again smite any more every thing living, as I have done. (Genesis 8:20–21 KJV)

Noah built an altar, as the world first needed to be cleansed, and then God made a covenant with Noah.

"When the bow is in the cloud, then I will look upon it, to remember the everlasting covenant between God and every living creature of all flesh that is on the earth." And God said to Noah, "**This is the sign of the covenant** which I have established between Me and all flesh that is on the earth." (Genesis 9:16–17 NASB)

The Lord gave the rainbow as a sign that he would not destroy the world again with water. Rather, he chose to redeem those in the world, so he made or described His plan to go forth, restoring man to his original state of being. The goal for His plan is stated in Genesis 9:6. He repeats, from Genesis 1:27, that man was made in His image. God intends to return mankind to the state of being that He created before the fallen nature became a reality because of sin. He simply said to Noah that He would redeem man from the evil that dwells within and change mankind back, as it was from the beginning. Jesus came to begin and complete that process.

And God blessed Noah and his sons, and said unto them, Be fruitful, and multiply, and replenish the earth. (Genesis 9:1 KJV)

Whoso sheddeth man's blood, by man shall his blood be shed: **for in the image of God made he man.** And you, be ye fruitful, and multiply; bring forth abundantly in the earth, and multiply therein. And God spake unto Noah, and to his sons with him, saying, And I, behold, I establish my covenant with you, and with your seed after you. (Genesis 9:6–8 KJV)

The Organization of God's Witnesses through the Marriages of Jacob

The calling of Abraham: Abraham was a type or shadow of God the Father in the organization of the two witnesses.

> Now the LORD had said unto Abram, Get thee out of thy country, and from thy kindred, and from thy father's house, unto a land that I will shew thee: And I will make of thee a great nation, and I will bless thee, and make thy name great; and thou shalt be a blessing: And I will bless them that bless thee, and curse him that curseth thee: and in thee shall all families of the earth be blessed. (Genesis 12:1–3 KJV)

Abraham was called out of his country and led into the country that we refer to as Israel. His very calling became a type or shadow of the lost being called out of the world to be with the Lord in a place that the Lord has prepared. Abraham was called to be the father of the chosen race of Israel. The chosen race was to be a type or shadow of the chosen saved. Abraham was, of course, both. God then made a covenant with Abraham.

> Not as though the word of God hath taken none effect. <u>For they are not all Israel, which are of Israel</u>: Neither, because they are the seed of Abraham, are they all children: but, **In Isaac shall thy seed be called.** (Romans 9:6–7 KJV)

And God said unto Abraham, Thou shalt keep my covenant therefore, thou, and thy seed after thee in their generations. This is my covenant, which ye shall keep, between me and you and thy seed after thee; Every man child among you shall be circumcised. And ye shall circumcise the flesh of your foreskin; and it shall be a **token of the covenant** betwixt me and you. And he that is **eight days** old shall be circumcised among you, every man child in your generations, he that is born in the house, or bought with money of any stranger, which is not of thy seed. (Genesis 17:9–12 KJV)

Isaac was a type or shadow of our Lord Jesus in the organization of the two witnesses.

And they said unto him, Where is Sarah thy wife? And he said, Behold, in the tent. And he said, I will certainly return unto thee according to the time of life; and, lo, Sarah thy wife shall have a son. And Sarah heard it in the tent door, which was behind him. Now Abraham and Sarah were old and well stricken in age; and it ceased to be with Sarah after the manner of women. (Genesis 18:9–11 KJV)

And the LORD visited Sarah as he had said, and the LORD did unto Sarah as he had spoken. For Sarah conceived, and bare Abraham a son in his old age, at the set time of which God had spoken to him. And Abraham called the name of his son that was

> born unto him, whom Sarah bare to him, Isaac. And
> Abraham circumcised his son Isaac <u>being eight days</u>
> <u>old</u>, as God had commanded him. And Abraham was
> an <u>hundred</u> years old, when his son Isaac was born
> unto him. (Genesis 21:1–5 KJV)

The sign of the coming of the Messiah was once again presented through the older son or older age of a person. Sarah's bearing Isaac at an older age is simply a sign that Jesus—the fulfillment to the sign of Isaac—would come at the end of the first witness, Israel, instead of at its beginning. The eighth-day sign of circumcision became a central part of the witness of Israel, as the goal for the witness is to lead as many as possible to be ready for the eighth-day rest period. Remember that in the New Testament they had a disagreement as to whether Jesus fulfilled the sign of the eighth-day circumcision or whether the sign should continue until the church would fulfill the sign.

Isaac, in the following Scripture, did not go to Egypt for provisions as a result of a famine. He continued to trust in the Lord and follow the leadership of God. God then provided for him. Jesus did not sin when tempted but chose to stay in God's will, as the fulfillment of this prophecy of Isaac.

Keep the number ten in mind, as later the meaning of the number one thousand will be presented. The first ten might be thought of as the knowledge of the cleansing presented through Abraham. Ten times ten would be the fulfillment of the cleansing for all those who established a faith relationship with the Lord before Jesus fulfilled the type of Isaac on the cross. The cross was the fulfillment of the cleansing, or ten times ten times ten—the finished number.

And there was a famine in the land, beside the first famine that was in the days of Abraham. And <u>Isaac</u> went unto Abimelech king of the Philistines unto Gerar. And the LORD appeared unto him, and said, Go **not** down into Egypt; dwell in the land which I shall tell thee of: Sojourn in this land, and I will be with thee, and will bless thee; for unto thee, and unto thy seed, I will give all these countries, and **I will perform the oath which I sware unto Abraham thy father.** (Genesis 26:1–3 KJV)

Jacob was a type or shadow of the Holy Spirit in the organization of the two witnesses.

And the children struggled together within her; and she said, If it be so, why am I thus? And she went to inquire of the LORD. And the LORD said unto her, **Two nations** are in thy womb, and two manner of people shall be separated from thy bowels; and the one people shall be stronger than the other people; and the **elder shall serve the younger**. And when her days to be delivered were fulfilled, behold, there were **twins** in her womb. And the first came out red, all over like an hairy garment; and they called his name Esau. And after that came his brother out, and his hand took hold on Esau's heel; and his name **was called Jacob**: and Isaac was **threescore years old** when she bare them. (Genesis 25:22–26 KJV)

"Twins" brings to mind that the first witness, Israel, would be followed by the witness of the church. Remember that Jesus came at the end of the witness of Israel in the context of the two witnesses. This Scripture, however, is simply understood to set apart those that will follow the witness of Jacob or follow the way of the world. The focus is on the organization of the witness to God's redemption plan through Jacob.

The Marriages of Jacob

The Lord revealed the organization of how the world would know of His redemption plan—and how it would be realized—through the marriages of Jacob. His plan would be communicated from the calling of Abraham to the end of the age through these two witnesses—the first witness through Israel and then the second witness through the church. These two witnesses are referenced in the Scriptures from this point on, until John finally references them in the book of Revelation.

Jacob was in the Holy Land when Isaac sent him to find a wife. Remember that it was Jacob whose name was changed to Israel to become the first of the two witnesses. Jacob was the type of the Holy Spirit, as the witness to God's redemption of man in the first instance is always the work of the Holy Spirit. Faith is responding to the conviction of sin that the Holy Spirit brings about in the life of those separated from God by sin. Just as Jacob left the Holy Land, so did Jesus come down to earth to bring about salvation to the lost who were separated from God's Holy Spirit.

> And Isaac called Jacob, and blessed him, and charged
> him, and said unto him, Thou shalt not take a wife of

the daughters of Canaan. Arise, go to Padan-aram, to the house of Bethuel thy mother's father; and take thee a wife **from thence of the daughters of Laban** thy mother's brother. And God Almighty **bless thee, and make thee fruitful, and multiply thee**, that thou mayest be a multitude of people. (Genesis 28:1–3 KJV)

Jacob was instructed to marry from the chosen race that began with Abraham. Marriage within the chosen Israel was a sign that the redeemed should marry only the redeemed, to keep the witness pure. Israel has been faithful throughout their generations to do this. They would marry and then wait one year, or fifty-two Sabbath days, before bringing forth life from the marriage. This was a sign of the Holy Spirit's bringing forth spiritual life for those who accept the Messiah at Pentecost. These marriages would occur in the world, where salvation occurs, and not in the Holy Land. The witness is *to* the world *in* the world.

And while he yet spake with them, Rachel came with her father's sheep: for she kept them. And it came to pass, when Jacob saw Rachel the daughter of Laban his mother's brother, and the sheep of Laban his mother's brother, that Jacob went near, and rolled the stone from the well's mouth, and watered the flock of Laban his mother's brother. And <u>Jacob kissed Rachel, and lifted up his voice, and wept</u>. And Jacob told Rachel that he was her father's brother, and that he was Rebekah's son: and she ran and told her father. (Genesis 29:9–12 KJV)

89

Jacob kissed Rachel and wept? Good grief, love at first sight. Rachel was to be Jacob's first choice from that moment on. Then things didn't work out for Jacob, according to Jacob's plan. They were to work out perfectly for God's plan. Jesus needs to be everyone's first choice. How, then, did it happen?

> And Laban said unto Jacob, Because thou art my brother, shouldest thou therefore serve me for nought? tell me, what shall thy wages be? And Laban had **two** daughters: the name of **the elder was Leah**, and the name of **the younger was Rachel**. Leah was tender eyed; but Rachel was beautiful and well favoured. And Jacob loved Rachel; and said, I will **serve thee seven years** for Rachel thy younger daughter. And Laban said, It is better that I give her to thee, than that I should give her to another man: abide with me. And Jacob **served seven years** for Rachel; and they seemed unto him but a few days, for the love he had to her. (Genesis 29:15–20 KJV)

Time goes fast when one is in love. Seven years—and what happened to Jacob's plan? God's plan was working out perfectly. The use of wine at a wedding was probably not a good idea.

> And it came to pass, that in the morning, behold, it was Leah: and he said to Laban, What is this thou hast done unto me? did not I serve with thee for Rachel? wherefore then hast thou beguiled me? And Laban said, It must not be so done in our country, to give the younger before the firstborn. (Genesis 29:25–26 KJV)

The sign of the older first and then the younger continues throughout the witness of Israel. The first seven resulted in a marriage to the older. The first witness was Israel.

> And he went in also unto Rachel, and he loved also Rachel more than Leah, and served with him **yet seven other years**. (Genesis 29:30 KJV)

Fourteen years—and then Jacob's plan and God's plan came together. Fourteen was the two sevens that brought forth the birth of Jesus. Jacob served a total of twenty years. Twenty, or ten (the multiple cleansing of the Lord) times the two witnesses completes the witness. The additional six years would end the witness to God's redemption plan at the second coming of the Lord; that is, at the third six, just before the blowing of the seventh trumpet or the third seven. The three periods of the witness to God's redemption plan end with a six. The last two begin with a seven. This is the same sign that was given by Noah when he sent out the dove from the ark.

> Thus have I been **twenty years** in thy house; I served thee **fourteen years** for thy two daughters, and **six years** for thy cattle: and thou hast changed my wages **ten** times. (Genesis 31:41 KJV)

Leah, the older daughter, became a type of the first witness, Israel. Rachel, the younger daughter, became a type of the second witness, the New Testament church. The births of the twelve sons help us to understand these two witnesses. Throughout the Scriptures the number twelve (or the multiple of it) always refers to the witnesses of God. Sometimes the Scripture refers to twelve in the context of these twelve sons; sometimes it's in the context of the twelve tribes or the twelve apostles. The twelve sons reference all the witnesses of the Holy Spirit, no matter when it happened. The twelve tribes reference the first witness, Israel. This difference is understood through the organization to the birth of these twelve sons. Read carefully as the following Scriptures are presented.

> The sons of **Leah**; Ruben, Jacob's firstborn, and Simeon, and Levi, and Judah, and Issachar, and Zebulun: The sons of **Rachel**; Joseph, and Benjamin: And the sons of Bilhah, Rachel's handmaid; Dan, and Naphtali: And the sons of Zilpah, Leah's handmaid; Gad, and Asher: these are the sons of Jacob, which were born to him in Padan-aram. (Genesis 35:23–26 KJV)

Notice that (1) six sons were born to a first wife, Leah; (2) two sons were born to Leah's maid; (3) two sons were born to a second wife, Rachel; and (4) two sons were born to Rachel's maid.

Six sons from the first marriage—the third son was Levi, who became the priesthood tribe. On the third day, Jesus arose, and the priesthood of the chosen saved became the fulfillment of the sign that Levi began. Six comes up short of the seventh-day rest. The seventh-day rest judicially did not become a reality though the first witness. Judah was the fourth son born to Leah. It was through the tribe of Judah that Jesus was born at the end of the fourth period.

There were two sons through the second marriage. Joseph was the seventh son born to the two marriages. He was the first born to the second marriage. Jesus was the firstborn son of God. Joseph became the type of the Christ when the witness of Israel began. The seventh-day rest became a reality at the beginning of the second witness. Rachel was the marriage of first choice.

Benjamin was the eighth son born to the two marriages. Rachel died when Benjamin was born as they were about to enter the Holy Land. Benjamin, the eighth son, became the sign of the chosen saved, when they will be taken up at the second coming to enter that place that the Lord has prepared for them. Rachel's death became a sign that the witness will end at that time, when the chosen enter the eighth-day period. Jacob left the Holy Land and now is about to go back to Bethlehem. The witness began when he left the Holy Land and will end upon his return in the sign of the two marriages. This parallels the time from Adam to the second coming of our Lord.

> Then they journeyed from Bethel; and when there was still some distance to go to Ephrath, Rachel began to give birth and she suffered severe labor. And it came about when she was in severe labor that the midwife said to her, "Do not fear, for now you have another son." And it came about as her soul was departing (for she died), that she named him Ben-oni; but his father called him Benjamin. So Rachel died and was buried on the way to Ephrath (that is, Bethlehem). (Genesis 35:16–19 NASB)

> Jacob said, "O God of my father Abraham and God of my father Isaac, O LORD, who didst say to me, 'Return **to your country and to your relatives, and I will prosper you,'** I am unworthy of all the loving kindness and of all the faithfulness which Thou hast

shown to Thy servant; for with my staff only I crossed this Jordan, and now I have **become two** companies." (Genesis 32:9–10 NASB)

Jacob's two marriages had become a sign of the two witnesses. At this point, Jacob had become two companies instead of one. Jacob would be identified only with the first when his name was changed.

Remember when Jacob left the Holy Land, the Lord said in Genesis 28:3 that he would become a company of peoples. That became a reality, first in the organization of the witnesses and then when his name was changed to Israel, the first witness.

And may God Almighty **bless you and make you fruitful and multiply you**, that you may become a **company** of peoples. (Genesis 28:3 NASB)

And Jacob was left alone; and there wrestled a man with him until the breaking of the day. And when he saw that he prevailed not against him, he touched the hollow of his thigh; and the hollow of Jacob's thigh was out of joint, as he wrestled with him. And he said, Let me go, for the day breaketh. And he said, I will not let thee go, except thou bless me. And he said unto him, What is thy name? And he said, Jacob. And he said, **Thy name shall be called no more Jacob, but Israel**: for as a prince hast thou power with God and with men, and hast prevailed. And Jacob asked him, and said, Tell me, I pray thee, thy name. And he said, Wherefore is it that thou dost ask after my name? And he blessed him there. And Jacob called the name of the place Peniel: **for I have seen God face to face, and my life is preserved**. (Genesis 32:24–30 KJV)

The four sons born from the two maids appear to represent the witness of the Holy Spirit; they are separate from or outside the two witnesses. There are three periods of the witness to God's redemption plan. The following Scripture contains the organization of the witnesses as they prepare to reenter the Holy Land. This is a type of the chosen saved entering into that place that the Lord has prepared at His second coming.

And Jacob lifted up his eyes, and looked, and, behold, Esau came, and with him four hundred men. And he divided the children unto Leah, and unto Rachel, and unto the two handmaids. And he put the **handmaids and their children foremost**, and **Leah and her children after**, and **Rachel and Joseph hindermost**. And **he passed over before them**, and bowed himself to the ground **seven times**, until he came near to his brother. And Esau ran to meet him, and embraced him, and fell on his neck, and kissed him: and they wept. (Genesis 33:1–4 KJV)

The first period of the witness: Adam to Abraham, as represented by the maids and their children in front of the line.

The second period of the witness: Abraham to the birth of Christ; Leah and her children second in line.

The third period of the witness: the first advent of Christ to the second advent of Christ.

The sign of the two <u>marriages</u> are in the same order as history has recorded the witness. Jacob, a type of the Holy Spirit, did not bring up the rear. The Holy Spirit goes first, leading the redeemed into the seventh-day rest and then the eighth-day rest at the eighth-day period.

For all those who have received redemption by ten—the multiple cleansing from sin by our Lord—times seven, the seventh-day rest will become the fulfillment of the sign of the two marriages, as recorded in the following Scripture at the end of the seventieth week of Daniel.

> And all the souls that came out of the loins of Jacob **were seventy souls**: for <u>Joseph was in Egypt already.</u> (Exodus 1:5 KJV)

The Witness of the Twelve Tribes of the Chosen Race of Israel

The Scriptures make it quite clear that Israel was the first of the two witnesses.

> **Ye are my witnesses**, saith the LORD, and my servant whom I have chosen: that ye may know and believe me, and understand that I am he: before me there was no God formed, neither shall there be after me. I, even I, am the LORD; and <u>beside me there is no saviour.</u> I have declared, and have saved, and I have shewed, when there was no strange god among you: therefore **ye are my witnesses,** saith the LORD, that I am God. (Isaiah 43:10–12 KJV)

The First Captivity

Jacob's name was changed to Israel, and then the first overview of God's redemption plan came through the first captivity of Israel as His witness. The Lord's plan was that the first captivity would become a visual type of the gospel. The Scripture records that it was 430 years before they were rescued. History records four hundred years of what was called the intrabiblical period. Four hundred, plus the life of Christ, comes to mind as a possible fulfillment of this prophecy. Notice in the following Scripture that it would end in the fourth generation. Jesus was born at the end of the fourth period. The number four hundred can be understood as four times ten times ten, or ten times ten, meaning the completion of the fourth. Be aware that this happens over and over in the Scripture. Ten times ten times ten means it is finished, rather than completed. Watch the Scriptures closely and discover that this seems to be consistently true.

> And when the sun was going down, a deep sleep fell upon Abram; and, lo, an horror of great darkness fell upon him. And he said unto Abram, Know of a surety that thy seed shall be a stranger in a land that is not theirs, and shall serve them; **and they shall afflict them four hundred years;** And also that nation, whom they shall serve, will I judge: and afterward shall they come out with great substance. And thou shalt go to thy fathers in peace; thou shalt be buried in a good old age. But in **the fourth generation** they shall come hither again: for the iniquity of the Amorites is not yet full. (Genesis 15:12–16 KJV)

The details of the first captivity are so extensive that this writing can only touch on a few. An overview in outline form will sum up thousands of details. Remember that this captivity is all about presenting the gospel. The Scripture that was given within this period, plus the visual sign of Israel, presented God's redemption plan, from the fall in the garden to the end of the age. Joseph interpreted the dream as seven years of plenty and then seven years of want. Adam and Eve experienced the fullness of the spiritual seven years of plenty. The world is experiencing the ongoing spiritual famine, separated from the Lord's seventh-day rest.

> Behold, there come **seven years of great plenty** throughout all the land of Egypt: And there shall arise after them **seven years of famine**; and all the plenty shall be forgotten in the land of Egypt; and the famine shall consume the land. (Genesis 41:29–30 KJV)

A Recap of the Events of the First Captivity of Israel

Joseph, a type of Jesus, was sent ahead into Egypt. Jesus was in the world before man sinned, and then He came born of a virgin to fulfill the sign of Joseph.

Israel and his sons chose to leave the Promised Land. Jesus did not choose to sin. Remember that Isaac, who was a type of the Christ, did not choose to leave the Promised Land during an earlier famine, and then the Lord blessed him. The organization of the twelve tribes, at this point, was the same as the twelve sons of Jacob. Later, Joseph's tribe was divided between Manasseh and Ephraim. The tribe of Levi became the priests to all of Israel.

Joseph had made arrangements for provision for Israel in Egypt, a type of the world. Jesus has promised to provide all the needs for all of His children in this world.

> And Israel beheld Joseph's sons, and said, Who are these? And Joseph said unto his father, They are my sons, whom God hath given me in this place. And he said, Bring them, I pray thee, unto me, and I will bless them. (Genesis 48:8–9 KJV)

> And Joseph took them both, Ephraim in his right hand toward Israel's left hand, and Manasseh in his left hand toward Israel's right hand, and brought them near unto him. And Israel stretched out his right hand, and laid it upon Ephraim's head, who was the younger, and his left hand upon Manasseh's head, guiding his hands wittingly; for **Manasseh was the firstborn**. And he blessed Joseph, and said, God, before whom my fathers Abraham and Isaac did walk, the God which fed me all my life long unto this day, The Angel which redeemed me from all evil, bless the lads; and let my name be named on them, and the name of my fathers Abraham and Isaac; and let them grow into a multitude in the midst of the earth. And when Joseph saw that his father laid his right hand upon the head of Ephraim, it displeased him: and he held up his father's hand, to remove it from Ephraim's head unto Manasseh's head. And Joseph said unto his father, Not so, my father: for this is the firstborn; put thy right hand upon his head. And his father refused, and said, I know it, my son, I

know it: **he also shall become a people**, and he also shall be great: but truly **his younger brother shall be greater than he**, and **his seed shall become a multitude of nations**. And he blessed them that day, saying, In thee shall Israel bless, saying, God make thee as Ephraim and as Manasseh: and he set Ephraim before Manasseh. (Genesis 48:13–20 KJV)

Joseph's tribe (Joseph, a type of Jesus) would become the tribes of Ephraim and Manasseh. Jesus was present in both the old and new covenant periods. Keep in mind that Jesus was only on earth in His humanity for a short time after he was born of a virgin.

The older would serve the younger in the following Scriptures. This becomes important to understand the Scriptures later on. Remember that Jacob was the younger, although not by much, as he the second born of twins.

And Joseph commanded his servants the physicians to embalm his father: and the physicians embalmed Israel. And **forty days** were fulfilled for him; for so are fulfilled the days of those which are embalmed: and the Egyptians mourned for him **threescore and ten** days. (Genesis 50:2–3 KJV)

Ten times four points to the fulfillment of Joseph as a type of the Christ at the end of the fourth period. Three score is three twenties. The witness is ten, the multiple cleansing, times the two witnesses. Twenty times three times simply means it is finished for all those included through the witnesses, which results in ten, the cleansed. It will be finished at the end of the seventieth week of Daniel. This same sign of the three twenties continues throughout the Scriptures in the original texts. It will show up in Solomon's temple, centered on the cleansing work of Christ.

Moses, a type of Christ, was called to communicate the release of Israel from captivity. Jesus descended to forgive those captured by sin and lead them into an abundant life relationship with Him.

The Passover set the captives free, when the tenth plague that God sent on Egypt was finished. Jesus fulfilled this prophecy on the cross, where He finished the work of setting His children free from the captivity of sin.

> "But do not be called Rabbi; **for One is your Teacher**, and you are all brothers. And do not call anyone on earth your father; **for One is your Father**, He who is in heaven. And do not be called leaders; for **One is your Leader**, that is, Christ." (Matthew 23:8–10 NASB)

God began to lead them apart from Moses from that day until they reentered the Holy Land. Jesus—and Jesus alone—will lead when one has chosen to receive God's free gift of salvation until His second coming.

> And they baked unleavened cakes of the dough which they brought forth out of Egypt, for it was not leavened; because they were thrust out of Egypt, and could not tarry, **neither had they prepared for themselves** any victual. (Exodus 12:39 KJV)
>
> **Seven days thou shalt eat unleavened bread**, and in the seventh day shall be a feast to the LORD.

> Unleavened bread <u>shall be eaten seven days</u>; and there shall no leavened bread be seen with thee, neither shall there be leaven seen with thee in all thy quarters. (Exodus 13:6–7 KJV)

Israel ate unleavened bread the day after the Passover, and it became an annual feast so they would remember. Jesus fulfilled the prophecy of the Feast of Unleavened Bread when He fulfilled the sign of the seventh-day rest on the day after the cross. Unleavened is fulfilled and then experienced when ones sins are forgiven.

> And Moses stretched out his hand over the sea; and the LORD caused the sea to go back by a strong east wind all that night, and made the sea dry land, and the waters were divided. And the children of Israel went into the midst of the sea upon the dry ground: and the waters were a wall unto them on their right hand, and on their left. And the Egyptians pursued, and went in after them to the midst of the sea, even all Pharaoh's horses, his chariots, and his horsemen. (Exodus 14:21–23 KJV)

> And they came to Elim, where were **twelve** wells of water, and **threescore and ten** palm trees: and they encamped there by the waters. (Exodus 15:27 KJV)

The Lord led the chosen to and then through the Red Sea. The Lord's cleansing prepared the church to be born again. Crossing the Red Sea was a type of Pentecost. The cleansing bowl outside the entrance to the Holy of Holies, which the high priest used before entering once a year, or fifty-two Sabbath days, was called "the Sea." The celebration of the completion of the reading of the Torah was held fifty-two days after the Passover, which confirms that they were at Mount Sinai for fifty-two days after the Passover. The Torah (the Law) was given at Mount Sinai within the first fifty-two Sabbath days, as the accounting of the chosen Israel was accomplished at end of that year. That accounting was a type of the judicial accounting of the chosen saved at Pentecost.

> Behold, the days come, saith the LORD, that I will **make a new covenant** with the house of **Israel, and with the house of Judah**: Not according to the covenant that I made with their fathers in the day that I took them by the hand to bring them out of the land of Egypt; which my covenant they brake, although I was an husband unto them, saith the LORD: But this shall be the covenant that I will make with the house of Israel; After those days, saith the LORD, **I will put my law in their inward parts**, and write it in their hearts; and will be their God, and they shall be my people. (Jeremiah 31:31–33 KJV)

The Lord unveiled Himself to the chosen after the cleansing of the sea through the Ten Commandments and everything else that happened at Mount Sinai. The sign of the image of God that would return to the chosen saved at Pentecost was given through the face of Moses as He came off the mountain. Moses was the one to whom God gave volumes of Scriptures that revealed God's redemption plan. The Lord's indwelling presence became the experience of the chosen saved at Pentecost. The Scriptures prophesied that the Law would be written on the hearts of the chosen saved.

The Lord gave instructions as to the details of the tabernacle that they built. This tabernacle was the center of the Lord's presence among them, as the Lord led them and provided all their needs. The tabernacle reminded them daily that they needed cleansing continually to stay in His will. The tabernacle was built with twenty boards, with each board one and a half cubits wide and ten cubits long on the north side and again on the south side. These boards were joined with forty silver sockets on each of the two sides. That is, these two walls were <u>thirty cubits long and ten cubits</u> wide. The west wall was made with eight boards. Six of these were one and a half cubits wide and ten cubits long. The other two were doubled corner boards that netted half a cubit wide and ten cubits long. The veil was ten cubits from the back wall, according to the historians Philo and Josephus. The tabernacle was then ten cubits wide by thirty cubits long by ten cubits high. The Holy of Holies was then <u>ten by ten by ten</u>. One thousand is used over and over in the Scriptures as the finished number of the multiple cleansing. The eight boards on the west side suggests that that finished number will occur for the chosen saved as the church enters the eighth period. Ten times three is the number that symbolizes the completion of the initial cleansing when one is redeemed. The forty sockets on the twenty boards prophesy that this would happen at the end of the fourth period; that is, Jesus did this on the third day. Certain numbers are at the very center of communicating the Lord's precious gospel.

> But Christ being come an high priest of good things
> to come, by a greater and more perfect tabernacle, not

made with hands, that is to say, not of this building; Neither by the blood of goats and calves, **but by his own blood he entered in once into the holy place**, having obtained eternal redemption for us. (Hebrews 9:11–12 KJV)

Jesus fulfilled the type of the tabernacle experience. Jesus leads the chosen saved daily, as His indwelling Holy Spirit continually reminds the chosen saved of their need to accept His cleansing from sin that they might walk in fellowship with Him and in His will each day.

There was also a golden lamp stand in the tabernacle that had seven lamps on it. The lamp was for light. Jesus is the Light of the World. The lamp stand sums up the number ten, the multiple cleansings times, and the number seven, the seventh-day rest. The cleansing symbolized by the washing in the laver between the altar and the tent by Aaron and his sons came first. Then the oil, a symbol for the Holy Spirit, would flow from the stand into the seven lamps, a symbol of the seventh-day rest, producing light, the symbol of the manifestation of the Lord through lives of the chosen saved. Jesus has promised rest for those who will come to Him. A partial summary of the contents of the tabernacle can be found in Hebrews 9:1–12.

This was the dedication of the altar, in the day when it was anointed, by the princes of Israel: **twelve** chargers of silver, **twelve** silver bowls, **twelve** spoons of gold: Each charger of silver weighing an **hundred and thirty shekels**, each bowl **seventy**: all the silver vessels weighed two thousand and four hundred shekels, after the shekel of the sanctuary: The golden spoons were

twelve, full of incense, weighing **ten** shekels apiece, after the shekel of the sanctuary: **all** the gold of the spoons was an **hundred and twenty** shekels. All the oxen for the burnt offering were **twelve** bullocks, the rams **twelve**, the lambs of the first year **twelve**, with their meat offering: and the kids of the goats for sin offering **twelve**. And all the oxen for the sacrifice of the peace offerings were **twenty** and **four** bullocks, the rams **sixty**, the he goats **sixty**, the lambs of the first year **sixty**. This was the dedication of the altar, after that it was anointed. (Numbers 7:84–88 KJV)

The numbers in the summary of the offerings of each of the twelve tribes, when they anointed and consecrated the tabernacle, continue to appear throughout the Scriptures. The list of what each of the twelve tribes brought is recorded just prior to this summary. Each of the tribes brought a silver bowl weighing "**seventy**" shekels. Each brought a gold pan weighing "**ten**" shekels. These numbers are surely entrenched in the Scriptures from the beginning to the end.

And Moses wrote all the words of the LORD, and rose up early in the morning, and builded an altar under the hill, and **twelve** pillars, according to the **twelve** tribes of Israel. And he sent young men of the children of Israel, which offered burnt offerings, and sacrificed peace offerings of oxen unto the LORD. And Moses took **half of the blood, and put it in basons**; and **half of the blood he sprinkled on the altar**. And he took the book of the covenant, and read in the audience of the people: and they said, All that the LORD hath said will we do, and be obedient. **And Moses took the blood, and sprinkled it on the people**, and said, **Behold the blood of the covenant**, which the LORD hath made with you concerning all these words. (Exodus 24:4–8 KJV)

Only be sure that thou eat not the blood: for **the blood is the life**; and **thou mayest not eat the life with the flesh.** (Deuteronomy 12:23 KJV)

Before the chosen set out to the tabernacle with the Lord, Moses gave them the sign of the blood covenant. The Lord required a blood sacrifice for sin, that justification from sin might be realized. The blood that went into the basins was then sprinkled on the people. Jesus gave us the Lord's Supper as a sign that the chosen saved might remember the new covenant. Compare the instructions with the Lord's Supper. Half the blood went to the altar, where burnt offerings were sacrificed to the Lord. The body of Jesus was sacrificed on the cross. Half the blood went into the basins. Jesus has promised continual cleansing from sin for the chosen saved who continually repent from sin. Moses sprinkled the blood (the life is in the blood) on the chosen people. The indwelling life of Jesus (the life is in the blood) became a reality to the chosen saved at Pentecost, when God's kingdom was restored.

And as they were eating, Jesus took bread, and blessed it, and brake it, and gave it to the disciples, and said, Take, eat; **this is my body.** And he took the cup, and gave thanks, and gave it to them, saying, Drink ye all of it; For this **is my blood of the new testament**,

which is shed for many **for the remission of sins.**
But I say unto you, I will not drink henceforth of
this fruit of the vine, until that day **when I drink it
new with you in my Father's kingdom.** (Matthew
26:26–29 KJV)

And when he had given thanks, he brake it, and
said, Take, eat: this is my body, which is broken for
you: this do **in remembrance** of me. After the same
manner also he took the cup, when he had supped,
saying, This cup is the **new testament** in my blood:
this do ye, as oft as ye drink it, **in remembrance** of
me. (1 Corinthians 11:24–25 KJV)

The account of observing the Lord's Supper in First Corinthians
reminds us of how life in Jesus is experienced. The Lord knows that
spiritual things simply do not come naturally to the carnal, fallen
nature of man. The sign of the Sabbath, or Saturday, was given to
remind the chosen, Israel, of the seventh-day rest. The Lord's Supper
is observed to remind the chosen saved of the abundant life. The
Lord's Supper is to be observed as often as you will, as is presented
in the Scriptures. The spiritual principle of the Lord's Supper is to
be observed spiritually as often as one needs to be cleansed from sin
that interrupts one's fellowship with the Lord.

The chosen Israel was in the wilderness for forty years. Jesus
appeared to the chosen saved forty days after resurrection Sunday.

The generation of Moses gave the signs, through the feasts, of the
first advent of the Lord. The generation of Israel that began with the
birth of Christ and ended at AD 70 fulfilled the sign of the generation
of Moses. The first three and a half years of the seven days of the

seventh week of Daniel for the sign of Israel became history, starting in AD mid-66 and ending with the destruction of the temple in AD 70. Remember that certain details of the first three and a half days were given in Daniel for this generation and that the second three and a half days were sealed up until the end time.

The Feast of Passover, the Feast of Unleavened Bread, the Feast of Firstfruits, and then the Feast of Pentecost are recaps of the witness of the generation of Moses; that is, the events of the gospel are separated from all the events of the exodus by the generation of Moses. The first three feasts were to be observed in the first month on the fourteenth, fifteenth, and sixteenth days. The Feast of Pentecost was to be held fifty days after the third feast. The Passover held on Friday, the fourteenth, suggests that Jesus would come on the second seven to fulfill the Passover on Friday, the sixth day of the week.

The generation of Joshua gave the signs of the second advent of the Lord as they crossed the Jordan and returned to the Holy Land. A second generation of the chosen Israel will fulfill this sign at the second coming of the Lord. Remember that Joshua, who was also a type of the Christ, was from the tribe of Ephraim. Caleb was from the tribe of Judah, which was the tribe that became the lineage of Jesus.

The last three of the seven feasts of Israel were to be held on the seventh month. The wilderness experience was a type of the church age; that is, the fifth feast, the blowing of the trumpets, was to be held on the first day of the seventh month. The fulfillment of this feast probably included all the angelical announcements, from the birth of Christ to His ascension. The sixth feast, the Day of Atonement, was to be held on the tenth day of the seventh month. The year of Jubilee was a type of Pentecost; that is, upon the fiftieth year, all the property was returned to the original owner. At Pentecost, all the chosen saved were returned to God. The trumpet was blown for the Day of Atonement on the fiftieth year of the year of Jubilee. The seventh-day rest became the experience of the chosen saved because the atonement of the cross became the experience of the chosen saved at Pentecost.

The seventh feast was the Feast of Booths. It began with a complete Sabbath rest on the first day of the week, continued on for seven days, and then ended with a complete Sabbath rest on the eighth day. Joshua's generation reentering the Promised Land is a type of entering the eighth-day rest at the return of the Lord. The chosen in the new covenant began to worship on Sunday, the first day of the week, or the day after the Lord fulfilled the sign of Saturday, the seventh day of the week. The feast continuing for seven days became a sign of the seventh-day rest experience of the church. The sign of the eighth day would also be on Sunday. Sunday becomes a sign each week of that eighth-day literal rest coming at the return of Jesus. Numbers 29 is an organization of the eight days of the seventh feast.

God used the <u>seven</u> feasts to outline the core elements of the gospel from the cross to the second coming of our Lord. Three more feasts have been added, bringing the total number of feasts that Israel celebrates to <u>ten</u>. How these three feasts fit into God's redemption plan may not be fully understood by this writer. They are Simchat Torah, Hanukkah, and Purim. It is interesting to note that they began with seven feasts and ended up with ten.

Simchat Torah: The Torah was given forty-nine days after the Feast of the Firstfruits at Mount Sinai. This confirms that the period from the Passover was fifty-two days, as the folks who started this celebration were at Sinai. Then the reading of the Torah was to be done weekly, with this feast celebrating the completion of the reading once a year at Pentecost. Remember that the crossing of the Red Sea and then the events at Mount Sinai were a type of Pentecost. This feast may have been simply a sign that at and after Pentecost, the chosen saved would experience the unveiling of God's will through their lives experiencing the seventh-day rest until the second coming of the Lord. Remember that the reading of the Torah was done at the completion of the rebuilding of the walls of Jerusalem, which was fifty-two days in duration.

Hanukkah: The history of this feast comes out of the Maccabees. The second temple had been desecrated during the reign of Antiochus IV. Hanukkah was known as the Festival of Lights and was celebrated at the rededication of the restored second temple. The menorah with its seven lamps was to be burned for one day. Someone pointed out that the account of what happened is in the Talmud, which this writer has not read. The oil placed in the menorah was enough to burn for one day, but it burned for eight days. The eight-day Festival of Lights was created to celebrate this miracle. A new lamp stand was created with eight lamps, one for each night of the festival and a ninth for what was called the *shamash*, or servant. The oil was placed in the servant and flowed out into the eight lamps. This lamp stand was called the *hanukia*. The hanukia is referred to as the menorah most of the time, but the name menorah is not correct in this case.

Notice that the Lord moved from the sign of the seventh-day rest to the sign of the eighth-day rest. The fulfillment of the second temple was the New Testament church, which will end at the beginning of the second coming of the Lord, as they enter the eighth-day rest and the eighth-day period. Hanukkah is celebrated at generally the same time as Christmas. Remember, Jesus was the first to experience the resurrection and the first to enter the eighth-day period.

Worship for the New Testament church is on the first day of the week, celebrating the resurrection of our Lord. The first day also has become a sign to the world that there is an eighth day coming. The sign of the hanukia in the second temple, a type of the church, became the sign of the eighth-day Sabbath rest that would be complete when the New Testament church age is completed.

> But the Jews who were at Shushan assembled together on the thirteenth day, as well as on the fourteenth; and on the fifteenth of the month they rested, and made it a day of feasting and gladness. Therefore the **Jews of the villages who dwelt in the unwalled towns** celebrated the **fourteenth day of the month of Adar** with gladness and feasting, as a holiday, and for sending presents to one another. (Esther 9:18–19 NKJV)

Purim: God used Mordecai, Esther, and the king, through a series of events, to gain the opportunity for the Jews to pursue deliverance from their enemies and then the victory over those enemies. The feast celebrating that victory is recognized on the fourteenth of the twelfth month. That's thirty days prior to the Passover. The use of thirty days for the month and the fourteenth day of the month points to the cleansing work of our Lord. That is ten times three, or thirty, and then the second seven. This may be a sign of the cleansing work drawing to a close, as it is in the last month of the year. Remember that the Passover was to be celebrated on the first month of the year, and the Day of Atonement came in the seventh month; that is, the final victory over sin will be recognized at the second coming of the Lord, as indicated by the twelfth month. Remember that Jesus came at the second seven to fulfill the fourteenth day date of this celebration. The <u>victory over sin</u> began at the Day of Atonement in the seventh month and will end with <u>complete victory over sin</u> at the end of the twelfth month, or month of Adar.

When the generation of Joshua crossed the Jordan into the Promised Land, the city of Jericho was to their right. The destruction of Jericho was the beginning of the purging of the Promised Land. The prophecy of this purging will be fulfilled when the final judgment comes on this world after the second coming of our Lord.

> And Joshua rose early in the morning, and the priests took up the ark of the LORD. And **seven priests bearing seven trumpets** of rams' horns before the ark of the LORD went on continually, and blew with the trumpets: and the armed men went before them; but the reward came after the ark of the LORD, the priests going on, and blowing with the trumpets. **And the second day they compassed the city once, and returned into the camp: so they did six days.** And it came to pass **on the seventh day**, that they rose early about the dawning of the day, and compassed the city **after the same manner seven times**: only on that day they compassed the city seven times. And it came to pass **at the seventh time**, when the priests blew with the trumpets, Joshua said unto the people, **Shout**; for the LORD hath given you the city. (Joshua 6:12–16 KJV)

The Lord gave this sign of the seven days, which would become the organization of the seven periods that will end with the second coming of the Lord. Remember that trumpets become announcements or communications from the Lord. Most of the time, angels do the communicating. Notice how often the number seven shows up in these signs.

They blew the seven trumpets as they marched around the city, once each day for six days. This prophecy of the first six days or six periods has been completed. Everything in the first six seals of the book of Revelation has been completed. They blew the seven trumpets as they marched around the city seven times on the seventh day. The events of the seventh seal of the book of Revelation are divided into seven separate divisions of time. At the end of the sixth division of the seventh period of time, or at the blowing of the seventh trumpet, the Lord will return.

Then they shouted, and the purging of the Holy Land began. The Scripture says that the Lord will return with a shout.

Remember that after the Holy Land was cleansed of all the kingdoms of this world, there was an organization of the dwelling place for the chosen. The Lord had a place prepared for each of the twelve tribes. Jesus has promised that a place has been prepared for all His children.

Through the prophet Daniel, the Lord referenced these seven periods and then gave certain details as to the beginning and end of the first four of the seven. Through the apostle John, the Lord gave more details of the seven periods through the organization of the seven seals in the book of Revelation. The information in the seventh seal, the time period, is divided into seven trumpets dividing that period into seven parts or seven divisions of the seventh period. Notice what happens in the following passage when the seventh angel sounded his trumpet. Joshua's generation shouted when they sounded the trumpets for the seventh time on the seventh day. The Lord will take the redeemed to be with Him, and the redeemed will shout from heaven as the seventh trumpet sounds.

> And they heard a **great voice from heaven** saying unto them, **Come up hither. And they ascended up to heaven** in a cloud; and their enemies beheld them. And the same hour was there a great earthquake, and the tenth part of the city fell, and in the earthquake were slain of men seven thousand: and the remnant were affrighted, and gave glory to the God of heaven. The second woe is past; and, behold, the third woe cometh quickly. **And the seventh angel** sounded; and there were great voices in heaven, saying, **The kingdoms of this world are become the kingdoms of our Lord, and of his Christ; and he shall reign for ever and ever.** (Revelation 11:12–15 KJV)

The seven feasts summed up the gospel, from the cross to the second coming of our Lord. The seven days, or seven periods, became a prophecy for a timeline for these events. Through the seven seals, John gave the information needed to identify these seven periods.

Solomon's Temple

> So all the generations from <u>Abraham to David are fourteen generations</u>; and from <u>David until the carrying away into Babylon are fourteen generations</u>; and from the carrying away into <u>Babylon unto Christ are fourteen generations.</u> (Matthew 1:17 KJV)

Before a review of certain numerical details of Solomon's temple are reviewed, it's interesting to notice that there are three major divisions recorded in the witness of Israel. These divisions are marked in Matthew's genealogy of Jesus by three fourteens; that is, at each event, the two sevens are present, prophesying that Jesus was to be born at the second seven. At the end of the second of the three divisions of time of God's witness to the gospel, Jesus was born. When the third fourteen appears, the genealogy was finished. When a number is the third throughout the Scriptures, it consistently suggests that it is finished.

What happened at the end of each of these three divisions of fourteen?

At the end of the first division of fourteen, David, a type of the Father, made the plans and provisions for the temple, and then Solomon, a type of our Lord, built the temple. Solomon's temple was a type or shadow of the cleansing work of the body of Jesus.

At the end of the second division of fourteen, three groups of Israel were taken at different times into captivity. Remember that the lost were or are in spiritual captivity within the three divisions of the witness to God's redemption plan. Then Solomon's temple was destroyed as a type of the cross.

At the end of the third division of fourteen, Jesus came. Jesus came to fulfill the sign of the first two divisions of fourteen at the second seven, or at the end of the second of the three divisions of the witness. The number fourteen to the third division was the <u>finished</u> work of the cross.

The details of Solomon's temple are so many that they cannot be a part of this writing. There are certain numbers within this temple that will be addressed, as they are very helpful in understanding how the Lord's redemption plan is communicated. Remember that there are only two temples in God's redemption plan. The first is the body of our Lord and Savior Jesus.

> Jesus answered and said unto them, Destroy this temple, and in three days I will raise it up. Then said the Jews, Forty and six years was this temple in building, and wilt thou rear it up in three days? But he spake **of the temple of his body.** (John 2:19–21 KJV)

Jesus was born of a virgin, not being separated from God except for that brief period on the cross. His body was the temple of the Holy Spirit of God.

The second is the church; that is, all the chosen saved. When was the last time you said to someone, "I have the Holy Spirit within me"? A child was given a picture of a church to color in Bible school. He was told to color the house of God. The child did as he was told but was heard to say quietly, "God don't live in no house."

> Jesus answered and said unto him, If a man love me, he will keep my words: and my Father will love him, and **we** will come unto him, and make **our** abode with him. (John 14:23 KJV)

> What? know ye not that **your body is the temple of the Holy Ghost** which is in you, which ye have of

117

God, and ye are not your own? (1 Corinthians 6:19 KJV)

And what agreement hath the temple of God with idols? for **ye are the temple of the living God**; as God hath said, I will dwell in them, and walk in them; and I will be their God, and they shall be my people. (2 Corinthians 6:16 KJV)

The organization of Solomon's temple, the first temple, teaches in great detail the cleansing work of the body of Christ. The Holy of Holies was twenty by twenty by twenty inside the holy place in the temple. When the three twenties are finished, the redeemed will be with the Lord. The Scriptures record that Jesus taught daily in the temple. Ten times the two witnesses to the third becomes a <u>finished</u> number.

I was **daily** with you in the temple teaching, and ye took me not: but the scriptures must be fulfilled. (Mark 14:49 KJV)

The choosing of David to be king:

Again, Jesse **made seven of his sons** to pass before Samuel. And Samuel said unto Jesse, The LORD hath not chosen these. And Samuel said unto Jesse, Are here all thy children? And he said, There remaineth yet the **youngest,** and, behold, he keepeth the sheep. And Samuel said unto Jesse, Send and fetch him: for we will not sit down till he come hither. (1 Samuel 16:10–11 KJV)

David was **thirty years** old when he began to reign, and he reigned **forty years.** (2 Samuel 5:4 KJV)

And the days that David reigned over Israel were forty years: **seven years** reigned he in Hebron, and **thirty and three years** reigned he in Jerusalem. (1 Kings 2:1 KJV)

The numbers seven and eight are included in this calling. David was the eighth son; that is, this is all about returning mankind to the seventh-day rest and then into the eighth-day rest at the second coming of our Lord. Notice also that David was ten times three or "**thirty years**" old when he became king. Thirty is a reference to the complete cleansing work of Christ. He reigned for ten times four or forty years. Remember that Joseph was thirty years old when he was put in charge of handing out the provisions.

Forty is a reference to the fourth period being completed at the Lord's first advent. The first seven years of David's reign were at Hebron over Judah. David and Jesus were both of the linage of Judah. David then reigned "**thirty and three years**" in Jerusalem over Judah and all of Israel. All of these numerical signs call attention to the temple that the Lord was about to build. The temple is all about the body or life of Jesus.

David was <u>seventy years</u> old when he died. Continue to notice that the sign of the number seventy (ten times seven) is consistently ingrained in the Scriptures. David did not build the temple; his son did.

And of all my sons, (for the LORD hath given me many sons,) he hath chosen Solomon my son to sit upon the throne of the kingdom of the LORD over Israel. **And he said unto me, Solomon thy son, he shall build my house** and my courts: for I have chosen him to be my son, and I will be his father. (1 Chronicles 28:5–6 KJV)

David did provide the plan and the provisions for the temple. God provided the plan and provisions for Jesus.

Then David gave to Solomon his son the pattern of the porch, and of the houses thereof, and of the treasuries thereof, and of the upper chambers thereof, and of the inner parlours thereof, and of the place of the mercy seat. (1 Chronicles 28:11 KJV)

A detailed list of all that David provided follows this verse in the Scriptures.

Solomon built the temple. The numerical signs keep pointing to the cleansing work of Jesus.

In the **fourth** year was the foundation of the house of the LORD laid, in the month Zif: And in the eleventh year, in the month Bul, which is the **eighth month, was the house finished** throughout all the parts thereof, and according to all the fashion of it. So was he **seven years** in building it. (1 Kings 6:37–38 KJV)

The fourth year: Jesus came to lay the foundation for building the New Testament church at the end of the fourth period. The house of the Lord will be finished when the Lord returns a second time as the church enters the eighth Sabbath-day rest period. Solomon experienced a great deal of trouble, giving the sign that it is finished. There were seven hundred plus three hundred problems; that is, wives and concubines that became a sign of the results of the cleansing of the temple. Ten times ten times ten is the sign of the finished cleansing work of Jesus. The thousand is divided in much the same manner as Jacob's sons, between those born within the sign of the marriages and those outside of marriage. The numbers seven, three, and one hundred (ten times ten) are used to total one thousand.

> David was **thirty years old** when he began to reign,
> and **he reigned forty years.** (2 Samuel 5:4 KJV)

David was a type of the Father. Solomon was type of the Son. God the Father made the plans and provisions to redeem mankind, and Jesus the Son carried them out. *Solomon's temple is all about the cleansing work of the body of Jesus.* That cleansing work would build the spiritual house of the Lord.

Some of these numbers are at the very center of the symbolism of the temple.

> And the oracle he prepared in the house within, to set there the ark of the covenant of the LORD. And the oracle in the forepart was **twenty cubits in length, and twenty cubits in breadth, and twenty cubits in the height** thereof: and he overlaid it with pure gold;

and so covered the altar which was of cedar. (1 Kings 6:19–20 KJV)

And he made the most holy house, the length whereof was according to the breadth of the house, twenty cubits, and the breadth thereof twenty cubits: and he overlaid it with fine gold, amounting to six hundred talents. And the weight of the nails was **fifty** shekels of gold. And he overlaid the upper chambers with gold. (2 Chronicles 3:8–9 KJV)

The size of the inner sanctuary has doubled from the tabernacle. Ten times two must reference the cleansing through the two witnesses. The organization of the divided number ten is consistent with this within the temple. Be aware that within Zerubabel's temple—that is, the second temple—the two witnesses have entered the holy place of God that was just outside of the Holy of Holies. Twenty times twenty times twenty would be eight thousand. The number to the third multiple is consistent with a finished number. Is it possible that eight thousand suggests that ten to the third will occur when the eighth-day period is upon the church?

And in the most holy house he made two cherubims of image work, and overlaid them with gold. And the wings of the cherubims were **twenty** cubits long: one wing of the one cherub was **five** cubits, reaching to the wall of the house: and the other wing was likewise **five** cubits, reaching to the wing of the other cherub. And one wing of the other cherub was **five** cubits, reaching to the wall of the house: and the other wing was **five** cubits also, joining to the wing of the other cherub. The wings of these cherubims spread themselves forth twenty cubits: and they stood on their feet, and their faces were inward. And he made the veil of blue, and purple, and crimson, and fine linen, and **wrought cherubims thereon**. (2 Chronicles 3:10–14 KJV)

There were two cherubim in the Holy of Holies in the tabernacle. The difference is the size and position of their wings. Each of the two cherubim had a wingspan of ten cubits. It's as if the Lord used these two to be types of God's use of angels communicating the gospel to and through the two witnesses. Five and five symbolizes the message to the two witnesses. The cherubims' images were also woven into the veil. Jesus was to become the veil.

And he made a **molten sea, ten cubits from the one brim to the other**: it was round all about, and his height was five cubits: and a line of **thirty cubits did compass it round about**. And under the brim of it round about there were knops compassing it, **ten in a cubit**, compassing the **sea** round about: the knops were cast in two rows, when it was cast. It stood upon **twelve** oxen, **three** looking toward the north, and **three** looking toward the west, and **three** looking toward the south, and **three** looking toward the east: and the sea was set above upon them, and all their hinder parts were inward. And it was an hand breadth thick, and the brim thereof was wrought like the brim of a cup, with flowers of lilies: it contained **two thousand** baths. (1 Kings 7:23–26 KJV)

123

> After this manner he made the **ten** bases: all of them had one casting, one measure, and one size. Then made the **ten lavers** of brass: one laver contained **forty** baths: and every laver was **four** cubits: and upon every **one of the ten bases one laver**. And he put **five bases on the right side** of the house, and **five on the left side** of the house: and he set **the sea** on the right side of the house eastward over against the south. (1 Kings 7:37 KJV)

> And Solomon made all the vessels that pertained unto the house of the LORD: the altar of gold, and the table of gold, whereupon the shewbread was, And the candlesticks of pure gold, **five** on the right side, and **five** on the left, before the oracle, with the flowers, and the lamps, and the tongs of gold. (1 Kings 7:48 KJV)

The cleansing bowl in front of the tabernacle was called a laver. The cleansing bowl at the southeast corner of the temple was called the sea. Remember that the crossing of the Red Sea was a type of Pentecost. The high priest would cleanse from this bowl before entering the Holy of Holies at the appointed times.

The dimensions of this bowl was ten cubits by thirty cubits. A college professor was once heard to say that these dimensions prove that the Bible is not literally true. The circumference of a circle is not three times ten. The Bible is only literally true when God has unveiled the spiritual truth of the Scripture. This Scripture is not about the size of the cleansing bowl but about the cleansing work of Jesus. Ten is the multiple cleansings that was shown to be a reality on the third day. Notice that there are ten times thirty gourds below the brim of the bowl—ten under each cubit of length, with the ten divided in two rows of five. The numerical details just keep repeating themselves. The bowl held how much? <u>Two times the finished cleansing number of one thousand.</u>

The foursquare organization of the twelve is repeated from the Lord's organization of the twelve tribes around the tabernacle. In the book of Revelation, John refers to the New Jerusalem as foursquare; that is, the chosen will come from all directions from this world.

To be born again, one must be cleansed by the blood of Jesus to communicate though the veil into the presence of the Lord. The high priests symbolized this as they washed in the sea before entering the inner sanctuary of the Lord every fifty-two Sabbath days. One's relationship with the Lord will never change once this has been experienced. Fellowship and walking in His will daily is yet another matter. There must be ongoing cleansing each day to stay in His will. The Lord's Supper reminds us of this each day that we walk with Him. These ten cleansing bowls, where daily sacrifices were prepared, communicate this truth. This cleansing is the work of the Lord. There were ten linen curtains in the tabernacle that prophesied this multiple cleansing. Only one cleansing bowl was part of the second temple. The redeemed must repent of each sin, one at time, to receive the multiple cleansings of the Lord. The ten lamp stands, each with their seven lamps, were divided as five on the right and five on the left. Each time the chosen saved are cleansed, the light of the Lord will shine through them as they experience the seventh-day rest.

The writer of book of Hebrews sums it up.

> But Christ being come an high priest of good things
> to come, by a greater and more perfect tabernacle, not

made with hands, that is to say, not of this building; Neither by the blood of goats and calves, but **by his own blood** he entered in once into the holy place, having obtained eternal redemption for us. (Hebrews 9:11–12 KJV)

Having therefore, brethren, boldness to enter into the holiest by the blood of Jesus, By a new and living way, **which he hath consecrated for us, through the veil, that is to say, his flesh**; And having an high priest over the house of God; Let us draw near with a true heart in full assurance of faith, **having our hearts sprinkled from an evil conscience, and our bodies washed with pure water.** Let us hold fast the profession of our faith without wavering; (for he is faithful that promised;) And let us consider one another to provoke unto love and to good works: Not forsaking the assembling of ourselves together, as the manner of some is; but exhorting one another: and so much the more, **as ye see the day approaching**. (Hebrews 10:19–25 KJV)

The Second Captivity of Israel

The beginning of the second captivity:

These are the people whom Nebuchadnezzar carried away into exile: **in the seventh year** 3,023 Jews; in the **eighteenth year** of Nebuchadnezzar 832 persons from Jerusalem; **in the twenty-third year** of Nebuchadnezzar, Nebuzaradan the captain of the guard carried into exile 745 Jewish people; there were 4,600 persons in all. (Jeremiah 52:28–30 NASB)

Three groups of people were taken into captivity at different times. The three periods of the witnesses to God's redemption plan come to mind. The destruction of Solomon's temple was a type of Jesus on the cross, when the sins of all held captive by sin would be set free. That temple was destroyed shortly after all three groups were taken into captivity.

In the **first year of Darius** the son of Ahasuerus, of the seed of the Medes, which was made king over the realm of the Chaldeans; In the first year of his reign I Daniel understood by books the number of the years, whereof the word of the LORD came to Jeremiah the prophet, that he would accomplish **seventy years in the desolations of Jerusalem.** (Daniel 9:1–2 KJV)

And it shall come to pass, **when seventy years are accomplished, that I will punish the king of Babylon**, and that nation, saith the LORD, for their iniquity, and the land of the Chaldeans, and will make it perpetual desolations. And I will bring upon that land all my words which I have pronounced against it, even all that is written in this book, which Jeremiah hath prophesied against all the nations. (Jeremiah 25:12–13 KJV)

And them that had escaped from the sword carried he away to Babylon; where they were servants to him and his sons until the reign of the kingdom of Persia: To fulfil the word of the LORD by the mouth of Jeremiah, until the land had enjoyed her sabbaths: for as long as she lay desolate she **kept sabbath**, to **fulfil threescore and ten years.** (2 Chronicles 36:20–21 KJV).

The captivity was prophesied to be seventy years in the Scriptures and was confirmed that it was seventy years by other Scriptures. Be aware that seventy years of captivity does not show up on some of the history charts.

The destruction of Solomon's temple:

"Now in the fifth month, **in the tenth day** of the month, which was the nineteenth year of Nebuchadrezzar king of Babylon, came Nebuzar-adan, captain of the guard, which served the king of Babylon, into Jerusalem, And burned the house of the LORD, and the king's house; and all the houses of Jerusalem, and all the houses of the great men, burned he with fire. (Jeremiah 52:12–13 KJV)

And in the fifth month, on the **seventh day of** the month, which is the nineteenth year of king Nebuchadnezzar king of Babylon, came Nebuzar-adan, captain of the guard, a servant of the king of Babylon, unto Jerusalem: And he burnt the house of the LORD, and the king's house, and all the houses of Jerusalem, and every great man's house burnt he with fire. (2 Kings 25:8–9 KJV)

The first Scripture records the tenth day, and the second records the seventh day. These numbers just keep appearing, but it's hard to know what happened here. Is one of these Scriptures in error or maybe not?

> And the king appointed them a daily provision of the king's meat, and of the wine which he drank: so nourishing them **three** years, that at the end thereof they might stand before the king. Now among these were of the **children of Judah**, Daniel, Hananiah, Mishael, and Azariah: Unto whom the prince of the eunuchs gave names: for he gave unto Daniel the name of Belteshazzar; and to Hananiah, of Shadrach; and to Mishael, of Meshach; and to Azariah, of Abed-nego. (Daniel 1:5–7 KJV)

> Then said Daniel to Melzar, whom the prince of the eunuchs had set over Daniel, Hananiah, Mishael, and Azariah, Prove thy servants, I beseech thee, **ten days**; and let them give us pulse to eat, and water to drink. Then let our countenances be looked upon before thee, and the countenance of the children that eat of the portion of the king's meat: and as thou seest, deal with thy servants. So he consented to them in this matter, and proved them **ten days.** (Daniel 1:11–14 KJV)

> The king answered and said to Daniel, whose name was Belteshazzar, Art thou able to make known unto me the dream which I have seen, and the interpretation thereof? Daniel answered in the presence of the king,

and said, The secret which the king hath demanded cannot the wise men, the astrologers, the magicians, the soothsayers, shew unto the king; **But there is a God in heaven that revealeth secrets, and maketh known to the king Nebuchadnezzar what shall be in the latter days.** Thy dream, and the visions of thy head upon thy bed, are these; As for thee, O king, thy thoughts came into thy mind upon thy bed, what should come to pass hereafter: and **he that revealeth secrets maketh known to thee what shall come to pass.** (Daniel 2:26–29 KJV)

The first four kings revealed: the first four of the seven kings of the book of Revelation are prophesied by the Lord through the dream of Nebuchadnezzar. These would become the four dominant kingdoms that could be recognized by Israel, which would result in the birth of the Messiah. Be aware that the dominant kingdom of the fifth king was the same as the fourth, according to John's information in the book of Revelation regarding the seven kings and seven periods. The seven kings represent the world governments in each of seven periods. God's redemption plan is all about His kingdom and not the kingdoms of this world. The seven periods began with the Babylon kingdom of Nebuchadnezzar. Nebuchadnezzar was not the only king of Babylon during the second captivity.

The interpretation of the dream by Daniel:

Thou, O king, art a king of kings: **for the God of heaven hath given thee a kingdom**, power, and strength, and glory. And wheresoever the children of men dwell, the beasts of the field and the fowls of the heaven hath he given into thine hand, and hath made thee ruler over them all. Thou art this head of gold. And **after thee shall arise another kingdom** inferior to thee, and **another third kingdom** of brass, which shall bear rule over all the earth. And **the fourth kingdom** shall be strong as iron: forasmuch as iron breaketh in pieces and subdueth all things: and as iron that breaketh all these, shall it break in pieces and bruise. (Daniel 2: 37–40 KJV)

The seven periods introduced by the generation of Joshua in Joshua 6 is revisited through Nebuchadnezzar. Sin is what separates one from God's kingdom. The Lord compares living separate from Him to being of unsound mind. Solomon said that it was insanity to live separated from God. In the first captivity, the Lord used the wilderness as a type of the spiritual condition of the world that the church would experience. Then He used the seven periods of time of Nebuchadnezzar as being of unsound mind to do the same thing from the beginning of the second captivity to the second coming of our Lord.

This is an evil in all that is done under the sun, that there is one fate for all men. Furthermore, the hearts of the sons of men are full of evil, **and insanity is in their hearts** throughout their lives. (Ecclesiastes 9:3 NASB)

At the end of **twelve months** he walked in the palace of the kingdom of Babylon. The king spake, and said,

Is not this great Babylon, that I have built for the house of the kingdom by the might of my power, and for the honour of my majesty? While the word was in the king's mouth, there fell a voice from heaven, saying, O king Nebuchadnezzar, to thee it is spoken; The kingdom is departed from thee. And they shall drive thee from men, and thy dwelling shall be with the beasts of the field: they shall make thee to eat grass as oxen, **and seven times shall pass over thee, until thou know that the most High ruleth in the kingdom of men**, and **giveth it to whomsoever he will**. The same hour was the thing fulfilled upon Nebuchadnezzar: and he was driven from men, and did eat grass as oxen, and his body was wet with the dew of heaven, till his hairs were grown like eagles' feathers, and his nails like birds' claws. **And at the end of the days I Nebuchadnezzar lifted up mine eyes unto heaven, and mine understanding returned unto me, and I blessed the most High, and I praised and honoured him that liveth for ever**, whose dominion is an everlasting dominion, and his kingdom is from generation to generation. (Daniel 4:29–34 KJV)

The spiritual condition of this world is likened to the experience of Nebuchadnezzar. The message of this passage is quite clear: don't wait, like Nebuchadnezzar, until the end of the seventh period to acknowledge the Lord. Remember that the Scriptures have declared that everyone will bow at the Lord's second coming and acknowledge Him as Lord. Nebuchadnezzar recognized the Lord and His kingdom but was not prepared to enter. Nebuchadnezzar's reign ended at the end of the seven periods and then—and only then—did he recognized the Lord. The "twelve months" brings to mind that the tenth feast would be held on the twelfth month as a sign of the second coming of our Lord.

This same sign was given through the doubting Thomas. Thomas came to Jesus on the <u>eighth day</u> of His appearing. Waiting until you physically see the Lord will be too late. Salvation comes through faith, for the Lord said that the blessing would come to those who believe without seeing. On the eighth day, everyone will see and recognize the Lord, but only those that have a prior faith relationship with the Lord will be saved.

Zerubabel's Temple

Be aware that this writer is not a student of historical dates and acknowledges that not all historians will be in agreement with these dates. Secular dates are used often to establish certain periods of history. The Lord's timetable may not match the following dates.

Solomon's temple was destroyed in the nineteenth year of Nebuchadnezzar's reign on the seventh day of the fifth month.

Nebuchadnezzar began his reign in 605 BC, according to a Baptist seminary history outline.

Solomon's temple was destroyed in 586 BC.

Fifty-two years later, 534 BC, could have been the date ascribed to the beginning of building Zerubabel's temple, as the first group returned to Jerusalem in 537 BC or 538 BC. The foundation was started in 536 BC, and construction began in 534 BC. Two years would match the two days that Jesus laid the foundation for the church before He became the firstfruits of the church on resurrection morning. Work was suspended in 534 BC until 520 BC.

The second temple was completed and dedicated in 516 BC. That is fifty-two years to the beginning of the building and seventy years to its completion. Fifty-two days after the cross, the church experienced the beginning of God's temple. Ezekiel's prophecy of this second temple calls attention to the second temple being the spiritual temple within in the body of the chosen saved. Ezekiel's temple had eight cleansing bowls, which prophesies the eighth-day sign within the New Testament church. At the end of the seventieth week of Daniel, the temple—that is, the church—will be complete.

Solomon's temple was all about the body of Christ. Zerubabel's temple was all about the body of the church. The ten cleansing basins and the ten candlesticks with their seven lamps were replaced with one of each in the second temple. The multicleansings are the work of the Lord. The chosen saved repent and seek forgiveness, one sin at a time.

Zerubabel's temple was remodeled a couple of times. Herod's work was so extensive that it became known to many as Herod's temple. Israel did not acknowledge it as Herod's temple, nor did they quit carrying out their appointed duties within the temple. Herod said that he was simply remodeling it, according to his words as recorded by the historian Josephus. Herod unwittingly changed the appearance of the second temple in the same way as the carnal nature of the chosen saved have influenced the appearance of the New Testament church in the world.

This temple was referenced as taking forty-six years to build, when Jesus said he would raise up His temple in three days. Keep in mind that the temple was built and then remodeled at least twice to create this number.

> Then answered I, and said unto him, What are **these**
> **two olive trees** upon the **right** side of the candlestick
> and upon the **left** side thereof? And I answered again,

and said unto him, <u>What be these two olive branches</u> <u>which through the two golden pipes empty the golden</u> <u>oil out of themselves</u>? And he answered me and said, Knowest thou not what these be? And I said, No, my lord. Then said he, These are the **two anointed ones**, that stand by the LORD of the whole earth. (Zechariah 4:11 KJV)

There were two olive trees, which are identified as the two anointed ones, added to the second temple within the holy place. The spiritual resurrection placed them there. Solomon's temple placed the chosen outside the holy place. In the book of Revelation, John identifies the two witnesses by referring to them as the two olive trees. The two olive trees were placed one on the right and one on the left of the lamp stand. The lamp stand had oil pouring out through the seven lamps; that is, God is pouring out His Holy Spirit upon and through the chosen saved. John makes that transition as he recognizes that the two witnesses have become two lamp stands, sharing Jesus with the world. The church is made up of branches that are grafted, enabling them to empty the golden oil from themselves.

But the court which is without the temple leave out, and measure it not; for it is given unto the Gentiles: and the holy city shall **they tread under foot forty and two months**. And I will give power unto my **two witnesses**, and they shall prophesy **a thousand two hundred and threescore days**, clothed in sackcloth. **These are the two olive trees**, and **the two candlesticks** standing before the God of the earth. (Revelation 11:2–4 KJV)

It is interesting and revealing to know the connection of the words "tribe" and "branch." Both Hebrew words for tribes[2] mean branch.

Zerubabel's temple was a type of the church and its relationship with God.

Rebuilding the Wall of Jerusalem

The following Scripture contains the prophecy of the decree to rebuild the wall of Jerusalem:

> Seventy weeks are determined upon thy people and upon thy holy city, to finish the transgression, and to make an end of sins, and to make reconciliation for iniquity, and to bring in everlasting righteousness, and to seal up the vision and prophecy, and to anoint the most Holy. Know therefore and understand, that **from the going forth of the commandment** to restore and to build Jerusalem unto the Messiah the Prince shall be **seven weeks,** and **threescore and two weeks:** the street shall be built again, and the wall, even in troublous times. (Daniel 9:24–25 KJV)

The decree from King Artaxerxes to Nehemiah to rebuild the wall:

> And I said unto the king, If it please the king, and if thy servant have found favour in thy sight, that thou wouldest send me unto Judah, unto the city of my fathers' sepulchres, that I may build it. And the king

said unto me, (the queen also sitting by him,) For how long shall thy journey be? and when wilt thou return? So it pleased the king to send me; and I set him a time. Moreover I said unto the king, If it please the king, let letters be given me to the governors beyond the river, that they may convey me over till I come into Judah; And a letter unto Asaph the keeper of the king's forest, that he may give me timber to make beams for the gates of the palace which appertained to the house, and **for the wall of the city**, and for the house that I shall enter into. **And the king granted me, according to the good hand of my God upon me**. (Nehemiah 2:5–8 KJV)

The wall defines the dwelling place of the chosen Israel. The Scriptures record that only about one-tenth of them lived in the city, so the city was symbolic or a type of dwelling place of the chosen saved. The second temple had been built but time passed, and the gates and walls had not been repaired. These are the same walls and gates that were around the city before the destruction of Solomon's temple. The record of the details of this reconstruction effort confirms the prophecy that it would be done in times of distress. The opposition to this effort seems to be at the very center of why it had not been done earlier. The second temple became a type of or was symbolic of the church. After Nehemiah submitted himself to God's calling, the Lord furnished Nehemiah with the materials and the authority to accomplish the rebuilding of the walls. The Lord continues to furnish the authority and resources to those who respond to His calling to build His church. Jesus is the answer and must be shared. Yes, there is great opposition and tribulation to those who will respond to this calling. The apostle John recognized this as the tribulation that began at Pentecost; it was almost the first thing he wrote about in the sixth seal of the book of Revelation.

Those who opposed Nehemiah had a painful awakening:

> So the wall was finished in the twenty and fifth day of the month Elul, in **fifty and two days**. And it came to pass, that when all our enemies heard thereof, and all the heathen that were about us saw these things, they were much cast down in their own eyes: **for they perceived that this work was wrought of our God.** (Nehemiah 6:15–16 KJV)

The number and names of the gates in the wall around Jerusalem may have changed in the different periods that the wall existed, but it is interesting that the number of gates was ten when the first temple was destroyed. Ten, the multiple cleansing of the Lord, became a reality on the cross; remember that the first temple was the type of the body of Christ. Fifty-two days were required to repair the gates and fifty-two days for the church to experience God's indwelling Holy Spirit at Pentecost.

The Gates:

> Then Eliashib the high priest rose up with his brethren the priests, and they builded **the sheep gate**; they sanctified it, and set up the doors of it; even unto the tower of Meah they sanctified it, unto the tower of Hananeel. (Nehemiah 3:1 KJV)

But **the fish gate** did the sons of Hassenaah build, who also laid the beams thereof, and set up the doors thereof, the locks thereof, and the bars thereof. (Nehemiah 3:3 KJV)

Moreover **the old gate** repaired Jehoiada the son of Paseah, and Meshullam the son of Besodeiah; they laid the beams thereof, and set up the doors thereof, and the locks thereof, and the bars thereof. (Nehemiah 3:6 KJV)

The valley gate repaired Hanun, and the inhabitants of Zanoah; they built it, and set up the doors thereof, the locks thereof, and the bars thereof, and a thousand cubits on the wall unto the dung gate. But **the dung gate** repaired Malchiah the son of Rechab, the ruler of part of Beth-haccerem; he built it, and set up the doors thereof, the locks thereof, and the bars thereof. But **the gate of the fountain** repaired Shallun the son of Col-hozeh, the ruler of part of Mizpah; he built it, and covered it, and set up the doors thereof, the locks thereof, and the bars thereof, and the wall of the pool of Siloah by the king's garden, and unto the stairs that go down from the city of David. (Nehemiah 3:13–15 KJV)

Moreover the Nethinims dwelt in Ophel, unto the place over against **the water gate** toward the east, and the tower that lieth out. (Nehemiah 3:26 KJV)

From above **the horse gate** repaired the priests, every one over against his house. After them repaired Zadok the son of Immer over against his house. After him repaired also Shemaiah the son of Shechaniah, the keeper **of the east gate.** (Nehemiah 3:28–29 KJV)

After him repaired Malchiah the goldsmith's son unto the place of the Nethinims, and of the merchants, over against **the gate Miphkad**, and to the going up of the corner. (Nehemiah 3:31 KJV)

An accounting of the chosen Israel was accomplished after the **ten** gates were repaired, which was a type of Pentecost. Remember that an accounting of the chosen Israel was taken fifty-two Sabbath days after they crossed the Red Sea, which was a type of Pentecost. John gave an accounting of the chosen saved right after Pentecost in the sixth seal of the book of Revelation. The following passage is just the beginning of the entire accounting. Twelve names are listed that returned from captivity. We can account for the total number of people but not from which tribe they come. The accounting at Pentecost was from the twelve sons of Jacob; that is, it included everyone who established a saving relationship with God.

And my God put into mine heart to gather together the nobles, and the rulers, and the people, that they might be reckoned by genealogy. And I found a register of the genealogy of them which came up at the first, and found written therein, These are the children of the province, that went up out of the captivity, of those that had been carried away, whom Nebuchadnezzar the king of Babylon had carried away, and came again to Jerusalem and to Judah, every one unto his city; Who came with Zerubbabel, Jeshua, Nehemiah, Azariah, Raamiah, Nahamani, Mordecai, Bilshan, Mispereth, Bigvai, Nehum, Baanah. The number, I say, of the men of the people of Israel was this. (Nehemiah 7:5–7 KJV)

The word of the Lord became available to the chosen Israel after the fifty-two days of the wall-rebuilding effort. They resumed the practice of reading the Torah, which was the eighth feast of Israel that began at Mount Sinai, where the Law was given. The events at Mount Sinai and the rebuilt walls were a sign of Pentecost, when the Lord wrote the Word on the hearts of the chosen saved.

So the priests, and the Levites, and the porters, and the singers, and some of the people, and the Nethinims, and all Israel, dwelt in their cities; and when the **seventh** month came, the children of Israel were in their cities. (Nehemiah 7:73 KJV)

And all the people gathered themselves together as one man into the street that was before the water gate; and they spake unto Ezra the scribe to bring the book of the law of Moses, which the LORD had commanded to Israel. And Ezra the priest brought the law before the congregation both of men and women, and all that could hear with understanding, **upon the first day of the seventh month**. And he read therein before the street that was before the water gate from the morning until midday, before the men and the women, and those that could understand; and the ears of all the people were attentive unto the book of the law. (Nehemiah 8:1–3 KJV)

On the next day, the Lord called their attention to the seventh feast from the first captivity. Remember that palm branches were used at Jesus's entrance into the Holy City before that final week. The "seventh month" refers to the first advent of our Lord. The fulfillment of this feast became the experience of the church, which started at Pentecost and will end at the Lord's second coming.

And on the second day were gathered together the chief of the fathers of all the people, the priests, and the Levites, unto Ezra the scribe, even to understand the words of the law. And they found written in the law which the LORD had commanded by Moses, that the children of Israel should dwell in booths in **the feast of the seventh month**: And that they should publish and proclaim in all their cities, and in Jerusalem, saying, Go forth unto the mount, and fetch olive branches, and pine branches, and myrtle branches, and palm branches, and branches of thick trees, to make booths, as it is written. So the people went forth, and brought them, and made themselves booths, every one upon the roof of his house, and in their courts, and in the courts of the house of God, and in the street of the water gate, and in the street of the **gate of Ephraim**. And all the congregation of them that were come again out of the captivity made booths, and sat under the booths: for since the days of Jeshua the son of Nun unto that day had not the children of Israel done so. And there was very great gladness. Also day by day, from the first day unto the last day, he read in the book of the law of God. And **they kept the feast seven days; and on the eighth day was a solemn assembly**, according unto the manner. (Nehemiah 8:13–18 KJV)

The "twenty-four" in the following Scripture may refer to the twelve tribes and the twelve apostles as they became one in the Spirit at Pentecost. The cleansing of those who confessed their sins was important, as it gave the Lord freedom to present the prophecy known as the seventy weeks of Daniel.

Now in the **twenty and fourth day of this month** the children of Israel were assembled with fasting, and with sackclothes, and earth upon them. And the seed of Israel separated themselves from all strangers, and stood and confessed their sins, and the iniquities of their fathers. (Nehemiah 9:1–2 KJV)

Know therefore and understand, that from the **going forth of the commandment** to **restore and to build Jerusalem** unto the Messiah the Prince shall be **seven weeks, and threescore and two weeks**: the street shall be built again, and the wall, even in troublous times. And after threescore and two weeks **shall Messiah be cut off**, but not for himself: and the people of the prince that shall come shall destroy the city and the sanctuary; and the end thereof shall be with a flood, and unto the end of the war desolations are determined. (Daniel 9:25–26 KJV)

Be aware that matching time elements with Scripture can be very hard to do and also can become confusing. Israel uses the lunar calendar, based the cycle of the moon. Dates in the Old Testament must be understood in this context. The calendar that the world uses is based on the cycle of the sun. The sun is the source of light that sustains physical life in this world. God is the source of all spiritual life in the world. The moon reflects the light from the sun. The chosen saved reflect the spiritual light of God's Holy Spirit. Israel had to reconcile these two cycles once a year.

History, however, calls attention to the fact that both of these calendars were not capable of fulfilling this prophecy. Scholarship has used a thirty-day month or 360-day year and called it God's prophetic calendar. Seven weeks calls attention to the same principle of the multiple number forty-nine, used to show completion before the fiftieth Jubilee year; that is, seven plus sixty-two times seven years, using a 360-day year, match the time from the decree to the Passion Week of the Lord. The Lord was cut off on the cross at the end of this week. This writer did not do this calculation, but is it possible that at the end of the sixty-nine weeks, there were seven days then to the cross?

The thirty-day month was used by Israel, even though the average lunar cycle day was less than thirty days. Ten times three were not the dimensions of the cleansing bowl but was the multiple cleansing work of Jesus. The Lord has used thirty to communicate cleansing and appears to have used it in completion of periods. Remember that the ark from the beginning of the rain to the ark resting on land was five months, but also it was recorded as 150 days. Surely that was understood when those Scriptures were read. The Lord used thirty days. Remember, it's all about Jesus.

> And Joseph commanded his servants the physicians to embalm his father: and the physicians embalmed Israel. And <u>forty days</u> were fulfilled for him; for so are fulfilled the days of those which are embalmed: and the Egyptians mourned <u>for him threescore and ten days. (</u>Genesis 50:2 KJV)

The Lord gave a sign at the death of Israel that the witness of Israel would become the New Testament church. Ten times four, or forty, marked the end of the fourth period. Ten times seven, or seventy, marked the beginning of the seventh-day rest for the witness of the church. Then the sign of Israel was marked by the three twenties plus ten. When the sign of Israel is complete at the completion of the seventieth week, the chosen saved will be returned to the Lord. Joseph, a type of our Lord, carried Israel back into the Promised Land, a type of place that has been prepared for the redeemed, for burial.

The Witness of the New Covenant Church

The church has been called to be a witness—the second witness—for the Lord.

> And he said unto them, It is not for you to know the times or the seasons, which the Father hath put in his own power. But ye shall **receive power, after that the Holy Ghost is come upon you**: and ye **shall**

> **be witnesses unto me** both in Jerusalem, and in all
> Judaea, and in Samaria, and unto the uttermost part
> of the earth. (Acts 1:7–8 KJV)

The Scriptures proclaim that Jesus came to seek and to save the lost. Jesus came to redeem the world and organized first the chosen Israel and then the church to be witnesses to His redemption plan. The church was called and then filled with God's Holy Spirit, who is the witness, so that the authority given to Jesus can be manifested to the world through the lives of all the chosen saved, so that all who receive Him as Lord and Savior will be saved. It is the power of the Holy Spirit manifesting through the redeemed that brings realization of the sin within the lives of the lost.

The Scriptures speak of the fruit of the Spirit that comes to indwell the lost when the baptism of the Spirit is experienced. God is love, so when His Spirit within manifests through the lives of the redeemed, God's love is experienced. Experience God's love, and receive the love for the lost as God has shown by sending His Son. Experience the joy of the Lord that exceeds any joy that is in the world. The church is ready to be a witness for the Lord when the Holy Spirit is allowed to manifest before all the lost to see.

> But the fruit of the Spirit is love, joy, peace,
> longsuffering, gentleness, goodness, faith, Meekness,
> temperance: against such there is no law. And they
> that are Christ's have crucified the flesh with the
> affections and lusts. If we live in the Spirit, **let us also
> walk in the Spirit.** (Galatians 5:22–25 KJV)

The fruit of the Spirit is the source of the power. When one's carnal nature manifests, power is lost. The fruit of the Holy Spirit, however, is not the same as the gifts of the Holy Spirit. The Lord organized the church by giving every Christian a spiritual gift, designed for service within that person's calling.

The church was empowered and organized by the Holy Spirit to be the Lord's witness.

When a child is born, that child must be taught many things. When someone is born again—that is, baptized with the Holy Spirit—that person needs to be taught about spiritual things. The organization of the church through the gifts fulfills many needs, but all of these things should manifest in a witness for the Lord. Children are born with talents. When someone is born again, spiritual gifts are given. Sometimes talents are enhanced by a spiritual gift. For example, some people have the talent of music, yet when they use that talent, the Holy Spirit does not manifest through that performance. If the Lord has added a spiritual gift to that performance, the Holy Spirit will manifest to all who hear through the power of God's precious Holy Spirit.

An organizational function of the church must be to prioritize help for the newborn Christian to discover the spiritual gift or gifts that have been given. Then a place of service must be identified, so that gift can be freely manifested to fulfill God's will in the life of that person and in the church.

But unto every one of us is given grace according **to the measure of the gift of Christ**. Wherefore he saith, When he ascended up on high, he led captivity captive, and **gave gifts unto men**. (Now that he ascended, what is it but that he also descended first into the lower parts of the earth? He that descended is the same also that ascended up far above all heavens, that he might fill all things.) And he gave some, apostles; and some, prophets; and some, evangelists; and some, pastors and teachers; **For the perfecting of the saints, for the work of the ministry**, for the edifying of the body of Christ. (Ephesians 4:7–12 KJV)

Having then gifts differing according to the grace that is given to us, whether prophecy, let us prophesy according to the proportion of faith; Or ministry, let us wait on our ministering: or he that teacheth, on teaching; Or he that exhorteth, on exhortation: he that giveth, let him do it with simplicity; he that ruleth, with diligence; he that sheweth mercy, with cheerfulness. (Romans 12:6–8 KJV)

It appears that the perfectly formed church will not happen until the Lord returns and the fallen nature of man has been forever removed. The Lord's organization of the church, however, is really quite simple. Each born-again believer has been equipped and has been called for his or her place of service. God has a plan, and each believer has a place with authority for service in that plan. Be aware that the word "committee" does not appear in the Scriptures. Do you think the twelve apostles were a committee? In the New Testament, the words "leader" and "leaders" have almost disappeared, even though they were used extensively in the Old Testament. Read the words of Jesus in these two Scriptures from the New Testament:

But **do not** be called Rabbi; for One is your Teacher, and you are all brothers. And **do not** call anyone on earth your father; for One is your Father, He who is in heaven. And **do not** be called leaders; **for One is your Leader, that is, Christ**. But the greatest among you **shall be your servant**. And whoever exalts himself shall be humbled; and whoever humbles himself shall be exalted. (Matthew 23:8–12 NASB)

But not so with you, but let him who is the greatest among you become as the youngest, and the **leader as the servant. (**Luke 22:26 NASB)

If the church is to be an effective witness for the Lord, every member of the body of Christ must be set free to follow the Lord's leadership and be free to allow the Lord to manifest His spiritual gifts as the ministry of that person's calling comes to pass.

7

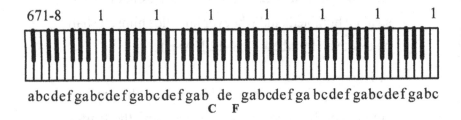

abc def g abc def g abc def g ab de g abc def g a bc def g abc def g abc
                              C F

Play C, D, E, and F as the first half of the seven days of the seventieth week of Daniel for the chosen Israel.

Start by playing middle C. Remember that the key of C was resurrection Sunday. Middle C might be thought of as resurrection Sunday halfway between the old covenant and the new covenant.

The note C is a full note, D is a full note, E is a full note, and F is a half note. There is no black key between E and F. You have just played three full notes and one half note. One does not have to use the black keys as half notes when playing something in the key of C to maintain the two three-and-a-half sequences that are fundamental to music theory.

The seven notes call attention to the seventh-day rest that became the experience of the church at Pentecost. The seven days of the seventieth week of Daniel reestablished access to God's seventh-day rest for the church. Daniel's words were "that a firm covenant will be made with many"; that is, the church.

The seven days of the seventieth week of Daniel were divided into two three-and-one-half-day periods for the sign of Israel. That is two three-and-one-half-year periods. In Daniel 12, the last three-and-one-half-year period was sealed up until the end time; that is, more attention was given to certain details of the first three-and-one-half years, as they were to become relevant to the generation of Israel that would begin at the birth of Christ and end at AD 70. This generation of Israel, beginning at the birth of Christ and ending at AD 70, became the fulfillment of the sign or type of the generation of Moses within the first captivity.

The first four kingdoms prophesied by Daniel became the first four of the seven periods that became a sign to Israel of the birth of the Messiah. The decree to rebuild the walls of Jerusalem that came later gave Israel more specific information on the first advent of our Lord. Keep in mind that the gospel has been continually communicated through historical events, feasts, and parables; that is, there were types or shadows of events given, that the chosen might understand the event that fulfills these types when they came to pass. For example, the Passover and the destruction of Solomon's temple were types or shadows of the cross. Be aware also that the books of Daniel and Revelation were written using a type of language designed to prevent the reader from understanding the content through a traditional literal interpretation. A certain knowledge of these types or shadows from the Old Testament are essential; John uses these so the chosen could understand, while the Roman government, in particular, would not be able to understand. Would the church have the book of Revelation if John had just called out the name of Titus, instead of referring to the beast of the sea?

A Summary of the Last Seven Years of the
Seventieth Week of Daniel

"So you are to know and discern that from the issuing of a decree to restore and rebuild Jerusalem until Messiah the Prince there will be <u>seven weeks and sixty-two weeks</u>; it will be built again, with plaza and moat, even in times of distress. Then after the sixty-two weeks the **Messiah will be cut off** and have nothing, and the people of **the prince** who is to come will **destroy the city and the sanctuary.** And its end will come with a flood; even to the end **there will be war**; desolations are determined. And he will make **a firm covenant** with the many for one week, but **in the middle of the week he will put a stop to sacrifice** and grain offering; and on the **wing of abominations will come one** who makes desolate, even until **a complete destruction**, one that is decreed, is poured out on the one who makes desolate." (Daniel 9:25–27 NASB)

The events of Daniel's prophecy in Daniel 9:25–27 are understood to be fulfilled as follows:

"Messiah will be cut off": The Lord will be "cut off"—that is, crucified on the cross—after the first seven plus sixty-two weeks from the decree to rebuild the walls of Jerusalem.

"the prince": The "prince"—that is, Titus—with Gaius began the siege in AD mid-66 and Rufus under Titus completed the destruction.

"destroy the city and the sanctuary": The sanctuary—that is, the second temple—was destroyed in AD 70.

"there will be war": It was destroyed with a military campaign of intense tribulation that lasted three and one-half years. It was so intense that it scattered Israel and the Christians to different parts of the world. Israel, as a nation or organized people, was separated from the entire Holy City until the six-day war in June 1967.

"a firm covenant": The new covenant became the experience of the church at Pentecost and will end when the final three and a half years ends at the return of Jesus. The seven days of the seventieth week was the beginning of the seventh-day rest for the church. The two three-and-a-half-year periods to Israel would become signs of the Lord's return. The first generation of Israel began at the birth of Christ and ended with a three-and-a-half-year tribulation period. A second generation of Israel will end with the final three-and-a-half-year tribulation before the church is taken out of this world.

"in the middle of the week he will put a stop to sacrifice": The sacrifices at the altar in the temple were ended as the second temple was destroyed.

"wing of abominations": The wing of abominations caused the destruction of the temple in AD 70 and will also cause the end-time destruction. Remember that Zerubabel's temple experienced a time called an abomination of desolation. This happened from 175 to 164 BC by Antiochus Epiphanes. It was a sign to Israel of what would happen to the temple. The abomination of desolation carried out by Titus was to Israel the fulfillment of the type of the first one. Then the abomination of desolation for which Titus was responsible became a sign or type to the church of the final event to be fulfilled at the end time. The desolation is simply a lack of the presence of the Lord in the temple; that is, in the lives of the people.

"will come one" and **"a complete destruction"**: The lawless one, known as the Antichrist, is the one who will be responsible for the final abomination of desolation that will bring the final judgment and destruction of this world as we know it. If you haven't noticed, Satan has been preparing for the lawless one at an alarming pace. The false prophet will also have had a role in this destruction. Remember that John prophesied that Satan would be released for a short time at the end of the thousand-year spiritual reign of Christ with His church.

The cleansing work of the Lord will be finished at the end of the church age. Ten, the multiple tasks of the cleansing work, times ten times ten finish the cleansing work of our Lord. The number one thousand in this context simply means that the cleansing work of Jesus has been finished. That same sign was introduced in the Holy of Holies of the tabernacle. The cleansing work of our Lord has to be finished to enter into His presence at the resurrection of the redeemed.

A Prophecy of the First Three and a Half Years

And **four great beasts came up from the sea**, diverse one from another. (Daniel 7:3 KJV)

In the book of Revelation, John recapped the destruction of the second temple after identifying what he was about to do by referring to the beast of the sea—that is, Titus, the one who is referred to as coming after the ten kings. Did the kingdom of Rome have ten Caesars or kings? More important is that the number ten calls attention to the period of the first advent of our Lord. Also, ten is the multiple number; therefore, ten may or may not be a quantitative number in this case.

Thus he said, The **fourth** beast shall be the fourth kingdom upon earth, which shall be diverse from all kingdoms, and shall devour the whole earth, and shall tread it down, and break it in pieces. And the **ten horns** out of this kingdom **are ten kings** that shall arise: and another shall rise after them; and he shall be diverse from the first, and he shall subdue three kings. And he shall speak great words against the most High, and shall wear out the saints of the most High, and think to change times and laws: and they shall be given into his hand until a **time and times and the dividing of time.** (Daniel 7:23–25 KJV)

The fourth beast was Rome. The sun had two basic functions in the creation account. Time was and is measured by the solar cycle, as one of those two functions. One time, or one solar cycle, is one year. "Times" was understood to be "dual," or two times. The term "time, times, and half a time" simply means three and one half years in this Scripture and in the book of Revelation. Once again, the fulfillment of this Scripture ended in AD 70.

The Lord Unveils Knowledge about the Season of the Lord's Return

And Jesus went out, and departed from the temple: and his disciples came to him for to shew him the buildings of the temple. And Jesus said unto them, See ye not all **these things**? verily I say unto you, There shall not be left here one stone upon another, that shall not be thrown down. And as he sat upon the mount of Olives, the disciples came unto him privately, saying, Tell us, when shall **these things** be?

and what shall be **the sign of thy coming**, and of **the end of the world**? (Matthew 24:1–3 KJV)

Jesus had just rebuked the chosen in the entire twenty-third chapter for their lack of commitment to their calling. Read the first part of this rebuke. At the end of this rebuke, Jesus said, "Your house is being left to you <u>desolate!</u>"

> Then spake Jesus to the multitude, and to his disciples, Saying, The scribes and the Pharisees sit in Moses' seat: All therefore whatsoever they bid you observe, that observe and do; but do not ye after their works: **for they say, and do not**. For they bind heavy burdens and grievous to be borne, and lay them on men's shoulders; but **they themselves will not move them** with one of their fingers. But all their works they do for to be seen of men: they make broad their phylacteries, and enlarge the borders of their garments, And love the uppermost rooms at feasts, and the chief seats in the synagogues, And greetings in the markets, and to be called of men, Rabbi, Rabbi. (Matthew 23:1–7 KJV)

Jesus then confirmed that the second temple would be completely destroyed. The disciples must have had certain knowledge of what the destruction of the temple meant, as they combined in their question three different events—not three separate questions for the three events that would come to pass at three different times but one question. This becomes extremely important when reading and understanding the Lord's answer to the question. Many times His answer will be directed at both the second temple and the church at the same time. The three-and-a-half-year period that destroyed the temple and other buildings became a type of the end-time three and a half years. In the book of Revelation, John understood this, as he recapped the first three and a half years for which Titus was responsible before presenting the end-time three and a half years.

It appears that the lack of commitment to the Lord will be both inside and outside the church. Both will contribute to the desolation that will result in His second coming.

Rome was the fourth kingdom of the seven kingdoms. Titus, the son of Vespassion, came out of the fourth kingdom, which was Rome. The prophet Daniel introduced four kings as beasts from the sea. In the book of Revelation, John refers to Titus as the beast of the sea. John refers to him as one who came after one of the ten kings of Rome.

The history of the destruction of Zerubabel's temple, according to Josephus the historian and as recorded in the *Encyclopedia of the Bible*, was that in AD 66, Gaius, under Titus, began the siege on the city of Jerusalem. Josephus said that it was not known exactly when in 66 the siege began, as his military campaigns were directed at multiple fronts. At the end of one year, Gaius could have walked into the city, as the siege was successful, but Josephus said that for some reason, he did not go into the city. Rome continued the siege under Titus, with Rufus destroying the temple in AD 70. The first time, times, and half a time prophecy came to pass.

The Lord's answer in Matthew 24:1–3 addresses both the first and second three and a half years. Therefore, it seems reasonable to continue this in the next chapter.

8

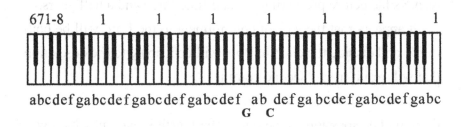

Play G, A, B, and C as the second half of the seven days of the seventieth week of Daniel.

G is a full note, A is a full note, B is a full note, and then C is a half note. You have just played three and a half notes. An eighth note was played to complete the seven full notes or fourteen half notes. The sequence of the seven notes began on C. Remember that the account of the resurrection of our Lord was presented when we played the first C. The first three-and-a-half-note sequence that began on C ended in AD 70. The second three-and-a-half-note sequence ends on C, or on the day of the resurrection of the chosen saved. The church will enter the eighth-day Sabbath rest period at the end of the third period of the witness that began with the second seven. Praise the Lord, for He will have come and taken up His church. Playing the eight notes is known as an octave. The gospel must have been known when music theory was established, for the Bible is inspired, not the piano keyboard.

A Prophecy of the Last Three and One Half Years

And at that time shall Michael stand up, the great prince which standeth for the children of thy people: and there shall be a <u>time of trouble</u>, such as never was since there was a nation even to that same time: and at that time **thy people shall be delivered**, every one that shall be found written in the book. And **many of them that sleep in the dust of the earth shall awake, some to everlasting life,** and some to shame and everlasting contempt. And they that be wise shall shine as the brightness of the firmament; and they that turn many to righteousness as the stars for ever and ever. But thou, O Daniel, shut up the words, **and seal the book, even to the time of the end:** many shall run to and fro, and **knowledge shall be increased**. Then I Daniel looked, and, behold, there stood other two, the one on this side of the bank of the river, and the other on that side of the bank of the river. And **one said to the man clothed in linen, which was upon the waters of the river, How long shall it be to the end of these wonders?** And I heard the man clothed in linen, which was upon the waters of the river, when he held up his right hand and his left hand unto heaven, and sware by him that liveth for **ever that it shall be for a time, times, and an half**; and when he shall have accomplished to scatter the power of the holy people, all these things shall be finished. (Daniel 12:1–7 KJV)

Comments as to what is heard from these Scriptures:

"thy people shall be delivered": The salvation of the redeemed will be completed at the second coming of Jesus.

"many of them that sleep in the dust of the earth shall awake, some to everlasting life": This is simply a prophecy of the completion of the bodily resurrection of the saints at the second coming of our Lord.

The lost surely should not look forward to the resurrection of everlasting contempt.

"and seal the book, even to the time of the end": Daniel did not give detailed information about the season of the second advent of the Lord. Remember that he gave the overview of the seven periods that began with the second captivity. Details about the last three and one half years were sealed up, only to be unveiled at the time of the end. The time of the end should not to be confused with the term "last days," as used in the New Testament.

"knowledge shall be increased": The first advent of the Lord and then the New Testament Scriptures provided that knowledge. That knowledge had been sealed up, to be unveiled by the Holy Spirit as the Lord's return draws closer.

"one said to the man clothed in linen": The vision of the one dressed in linen identifies with Joshua, who was a type of the Lord crossing the River Jordan. The Lord will be waiting at the river to take the last of the chosen saved across. The linen curtains, the linen found in the tomb, and the linen of the Lord's righteousness in the book of Revelation all point to the cleansing of all those whom the Lord will meet at the river.

"How long shall it be to the end of these wonders": The man clothed in linen answered the question. Jesus did know something about the season of His return. He did not know the day or hour.

"**ever that it shall be for a time, times, and an half**": The last three-and-a-half-year tribulation will scatter the power of the holy people, and then it will be finished. There will be a resurrection of the chosen saved at the end of this three-and-a-half-year tribulation period.

The Lord Unveils Details about the Last Three and One Half Years of the Seventy Weeks of Daniel

The Lord answered the three-part question in Matthew 24:3— one question about three different events. His answer was to inform the elect about the season of the Lord's return. In the following passage, the Lord separates His answer into two parts. The first is to recognize the season of the Lord's return, and the second is to make it quite clear that the elect will not know the day or the hour.

> As He was sitting on the Mount of Olives, the disciples came to Him privately, saying, "Tell us, when will **these things** happen, and what will be the **sign of Your coming**, and of the **end of the age?**" (Matthew 24:3 NASB)

The Question:

"**these things**": They had just been looking at the second temple that was a type or shadow of the church. Jesus said that it would be destroyed. The destruction was complete in AD 70. Keep in mind as this passage of Scripture is reviewed that the Lord used types and shadows to present His redemption plan, over and over throughout the witness of Israel.

"sign of Your coming": Israel was an organized people in the Holy City until AD 70, and this temple was a type or shadow of the church. These two three-and-a-half-year periods are tied to Israel as the sign of the Lord's return. Israel was in the Holy City as an organized people when the temple was destroyed, and Israel is back in the Holy City as an organized people now. The disciples knew there was a connection, as they only asked one question. Remember in the prophecy that the holy people would be scattered at the destruction of the temple.

"end of the age?": The first three-and-a-half-year tribulation was directed at both Israel and the church.

The destruction of the temple was a type of the final tribulation being directed at both Christians and Israel. At the end of the second three-and-a-half-year period, the Lord will return to take the chosen saved out of this world. The redeemed are judged and then placed in that place that has been prepared for them. The intense judgment on this world will take place, beginning as soon as the chosen are taken to be with the Lord. Ezekiel calls this period, after the bodily resurrection, seven years. John divides this judgment into seven events. The judgment of those separated from God for eternity will come, followed by the end of the age.

> And Jesus answered and said to them, "See to it that no one misleads you. For many will come in My name, saying, 'I am the Christ,' and will mislead many. "You will be hearing of wars and rumors of wars. See that you are not frightened, for those things must take place, but that is not yet the end. For nation will rise against nation, and kingdom against kingdom, and in various places there will be famines

and earthquakes. But **all these things are merely the beginning of birth pangs.** Then they will **deliver you to tribulation**, and will kill you, and **you will be hated by all nations** because of My name. At that time **many will fall away** and will betray one another and hate one another. Many false prophets will arise and will mislead many. Because lawlessness is increased, **most people's love will grow cold.** But the **one who endures to the end**, he will be saved." (Matthew 24:4–13 NASB)

The Lord's answer: Matthew 24:4–13

"all these things are merely the beginning of birth pangs": False teachers and wars will manifest throughout the church age while the Lord is saving His elect. It's interesting that the Lord calls these things "birth pangs," given that His work is to accomplish the new birth within His elect. Jesus said, You must be born again.

"delivered to tribulation": A three-and-a-half-year tribulation that scattered the elect when it ended with the destruction of the second temple. Keep in mind that the apostle John experienced this tribulation period. This tribulation was a type of the last three-and-a-half-year tribulation before the second coming of our Lord. The last three-and-a-half-year tribulation will simply be the beginning of the tribulation that will bring judgment on the world, right after the church is taken to be with the Lord.

"hated by all nations because of my name": Israel, the chosen saved, had become one with the church in Christ spiritually at Pentecost, and both are the Lord's witness. The elect were the target of the first three-and-a-half-year tribulation and will be the same in the second three and a half years.

"many will fall away": The Scriptures proclaim that many or even millions will be deceived, and many will have not responded to the Holy Spirit's invitation to redemption. The Lord rebuked Israel for failing to do God's will before the temple and city were destroyed. The more important question now is, what about the church? Winning the lost is at the very center of what the witness of the church is all about.

"most people's love will grow cold": Was love the dominating force when the second temple was destroyed, and is it today?

"one who endures to the end": The salvation of the chosen saved will be complete at the resurrection, when the Lord returns. Praise the Lord that He has promised to keep those safe who have been born again until that day.

> This **gospel of the kingdom shall be preached in the whole world** as a testimony to all the nations, and then the end will come. **therefore when you see the abomination of desolation** which was spoken of through Daniel the prophet, standing in the holy place (let the reader understand), then **those who are in Judea must flee to the mountains**. Whoever is on the housetop must not go down to get the things out that are in his house. Whoever is in the field must not turn back to get his cloak. But woe to those who are pregnant and to those who are nursing babies in those days! But pray that your flight will not be in the winter, or on a Sabbath. For then there **will be a great tribulation**, such as has not occurred since the beginning of the world until now, nor ever will.

Unless those days had been cut short, no life would have been saved; **but for the sake of the elect those days will be cut short.** Then if anyone says to you, 'Behold, here is the Christ,' or There He is,' do not believe him. For false Christs and false prophets will arise and will show great signs and wonders, so as to mislead, if possible, even the elect. Behold, I have told you in advance. So if they say to you, 'Behold, He is in the wilderness,' do not go out, or, 'Behold, He is in the inner rooms,' do not believe them. For just as the lightning comes from the east, and flashes even to the west, so shall the coming of the Son of Man be. Wherever the corpse is, there the vultures will gather. But immediately **after the tribulation of those days** the sun will be darkened, and the moon will not give its light, and the stars will fall from the sky, and the powers of the heavens will be shaken, and then the **sign of the Son of Man** will appear in the sky, and then all the tribes of the earth will mourn, and **they will see the Son of Man coming on the clouds of the sky** with power and great glory. And He will send forth His angels with **a great trumpet** and they **will gather together His elect** from the four winds, from one end of the sky to the other. (Matthew 24:14–31 NASB)

The Lord's answer: Matthew 24:4–31 continued.

"gospel of the kingdom shall be preached in the whole world": New folks are being born every day who need to hear the gospel. This witness will not be finished until the Lord's return.

"therefore when you see the abomination of desolation": The desolation of the temple was a type of the end-time desolation. Sodom and Gomorrah was a type of the end-time judgment on the world. Remember the conversation that Abraham had with the Lord? They finally settled on <u>ten</u> as the number of folks who would need to be found in the land that had established a faith relationship with the Lord to prevent the destruction that came upon Sodom and Gomorrah. There were not ten who had a faith relationship with the Lord, which would result in their sins being cleansed by the blood of Jesus. The land was spiritually desolate. The Lord knew this then, and he knows what it will be like at His return. The number ten was simply a sign of the need of the Lord's cleansing.

"will be a great tribulation": There is a tribulation approaching as the season of the Lord's return draws near. The last three and a half years will be completed to end this tribulation.

"but for the sake of the elect those days will be cut short": The Lord will return and take up His children to be with Him before the tribulation becomes the judgment on this world. Israel fleeing to the mountains at the destruction of the second temple was a type of the chosen living being taken up at the Lord's return.

"for the tribulation of those days": This tribulation will warn both the saved and the unsaved of the second coming of the Lord and the end of the age when this tribulation ends for the chosen saved.

"sign of the Son of Man" and "they will see the son of man coming on the clouds of the sky": The sign that is the second part of the disciples' question was answered in a way that everyone will clearly understand that Jesus is Lord on that day.

"a great trumpet": The writer of the book of Corinthians calls this trumpet the last trumpet. In the book of Revelation, John calls this trumpet the seventh trumpet after the seven trumpets that were blown on each of the seven times around Jericho on the seventh day. That seventh trumpet will be blown as the last three and a half years of the seventieth week of Daniel ends and the judgment on this world begins. Jesus said that the angels will blow the trumpet. John uses seven angels to blow the trumpet that divide the seventh period into seven divisions of time.

"**they will gather together His elect**": That's a lot of people to gather together. There must be a lot of angels. How can this happen? Once one is born again, a certain level of understanding of spiritual things comes from the Lord. Understanding it all will come when the elect or redeemed experience this event. Do you have your wings yet, and have you been practicing flying?

> Now learn a parable of the fig tree; When his branch is yet tender, and putteth forth leaves, ye know that summer is nigh: **So likewise ye, when ye shall see all these things, know that it is near, even at the doors**. Verily I say unto you, **This generation shall not pass**, till all these things be fulfilled. (Matthew 24:32–34 KJV)

What are all the things the Lord has been talking about? Observing all the people in the world becoming desolate from the indwelling Holy Spirit is the most dominant sign that the second coming of our Lord is at hand. The signs that point to the return of our Lord will be evident and should be recognized by the church.

Remember that in Israel's first overview of the gospel, the generation of Moses gave the sign of the first advent of our Lord. The fulfillment of this type or shadow was the generation of Israel that began at the birth of Christ and ended in AD 70. A second generation of Joshua was set apart that gave the sign of the Lord's return as they entered into the Holy Land. Could the fulfillment of this second generation also be seventy years? Seventy was a quantitative number when the temple was destroyed, while at the same time it called attention to the seventy weeks of Daniel. It certainly wouldn't be wise to do a calculation, as there is nothing in the Scripture that keeps the Lord from coming back today. Keep in mind that the last tribulation is assumed to be easy to recognize, but in fact, we only understand in part, as the Scripture says.

The day and hour of the Lord's return:

> **But of that day and hour knoweth no man**, no, not the angels of heaven, but my Father only. (Matthew 24:36 KJV)

There simply is nothing in the Scripture that allows us to know the day or hour. Do you suppose that it will be on the seventh day of the week; or on the first day, when the faithful are in church; or maybe on the eighth day? We do know, that it will happen without warning, just as in the days of Noah. Are you ready?

In the Book of Revelation, John Continues the Unsealing of the Last Three and One-Half Days

Through John, the Lord gave us information in the book of Revelation that helps to unveil the last three periods. Remember that this writing is simply a testimony of what has been heard (and is being heard) from the Scriptures. The review of these seven periods will be brief, with the goal centered on the meaning of certain numbers.

The first four seals review the first four of the seven periods. These seven periods will be complete when the judgment of this world is complete, or at the end of the age.

Limiting this writing to numbers that are used in the seven seals is hard to do, separate from the context of all of John's writing. A review of the seven seals, however, seems essential to the understanding of the context of the last three and a half years of the seventieth week of Daniel. Keep in mind that it is hard to keep focused on all that is known beforehand about the gospel when reading the book of Revelation, because of the symbolic language used. John adds at the end of his writing that nothing should be added to its content. Perhaps the Lord led John to do this, as He knew that certain "literal" interpretations could add to His redemption plan. It is exciting, however, to realize that the Lord often unveils the understanding of the redemptive work, as it is understood and implemented from the presence of God. Notice these two things from Revelation 4 and 5.

> After this I looked, and, behold, a door was opened in heaven: and the first voice which I heard was as it were of a trumpet talking with me; which said, Come up hither, and I will shew thee things which must be hereafter. And immediately **I was in the spirit**: and, behold, a throne was set in heaven, and one sat on the throne. (Revelation 4:1–2 KJV)

"**I was in the Spirit**": The presence of the Holy Spirit in the life of the redeemed makes communication with God possible. The Lord certainly had a very special calling for John as he experienced a vision of things to come.

> And they sung a new song, saying, **Thou art worthy to take the book, and to open the seals** thereof: for thou wast slain, and hast redeemed us to God by thy blood out of every kindred, and tongue, and people, and nation; **And hast made us unto our God kings and priests: and we shall reign on the earth.** (Revelation 5:9–10 KJV)

"**Thou art worthy to take the book, and to open the seals**": Jesus has the authority and knows all about what has taken place and will take place throughout the seven periods.

"**And hast made us unto our God kings and priests: and we shall reign on the earth**": The priesthood of the believer became the experience of the chosen saved at Pentecost. The Lord's kingdom was reestablished at Pentecost. Jesus will lead and would that all His chosen saved choose to reign with Him. He has a place for each of His church to serve with Him.

The first four seals, or periods, of the seven periods. (Revelation 6:1–8)

> And I saw when the Lamb opened **one of the seals**, and I heard, as it were the noise of thunder, one of **the four beasts** saying, Come and see. And I saw, and behold a **white horse**: and he that sat on him had a bow; and a crown was given unto him: and he went forth conquering, and to conquer. And when he had opened the second seal, I heard the second beast say, Come and see. And there went out another **horse that was red**: and power was given to him that sat thereon

to take peace from the earth, and that they should kill one another: and there was given unto him a great sword. And when he had opened the third seal, I heard the third beast say, Come and see. And I beheld, and lo **a black horse**; and he that sat on him had a pair of balances in his hand. And I heard a voice in the midst of the four beasts say, A measure of wheat for a penny, and three measures of barley for a penny; and see thou hurt not the oil and the wine. And when he had opened the fourth seal, I heard the voice of the fourth beast say, Come and see. And I looked, and behold **a pale horse**: and his name that sat on him was Death, and Hell followed with him. And power was given unto them over the fourth part of the earth, to kill with sword, and with hunger, and with death, and with the beasts of the earth. (Revelation 6:1–8 KJV)

The first four periods are defined by the four kingdoms. The Babylon kingdom was the first, then the Mede-Persian, then the Grecian kingdom, and then the kingdom of Rome. They were dominating kingdoms that were signposts to Israel to help understand the first advent of the Lord. In the context of the seven periods, they simply represent the civil governments of the world that existed in the world within each period; that is, four periods of civil government. In Revelation, John reviewed the history of these four periods of civil government with a few details of the circumstances of those times.

I saw by night, and behold a man riding upon a red horse, and he stood among the myrtle trees that were

> in the bottom; and behind him were there red horses,
> speckled, and white. (Zechariah 1:8 KJV)

> In the first chariot were red horses; and in the second
> chariot black horses; And in the third chariot white
> horses; and in the fourth chariot grisled and bay
> horses. (Zechariah 6:2–3 KJV)

John used the four different colored horses that he got from Zechariah. John knew and understood the white, red, black, and ashen-colored horses, but he couldn't call out Rome, so he identified the four kingdoms by referring to Zechariah's vision. The colors match, but the order of the colors are not the same. This writer will have to add this one to the large bucket list of questions for the Lord.

For whatever reason, the Lord did not include definitive information about the work of redemption within these four periods. The reason could be that Revelation centers first on the season of the Lord's return and then on the judgments that are yet to come.

The fifth seal is a brief recap of the fifth of the seven periods.

> And **when he had opened the fifth seal**, I saw under
> the altar the souls of them that were slain for the word
> of God, and for the testimony which they held: And
> they cried with a loud voice, saying, **How long**, O
> Lord, holy and true, dost thou not judge and avenge
> our blood on them that dwell on the earth? And **white
> robes were given unto every one of them**; and it
> was said unto them, that **they should rest** yet for a
> little season, until their fellow servants also and their

brethren, that should be killed as they were, should be fulfilled. (Revelation 6:9–11 KJV)

While writing the book of Revelation, John was located on the Isle of Patmos as a result of the intense tribulation. John wrote what the Lord shared with him to answer the question of how long before the judgment. This fifth period included Pentecost, as the chosen had received their white robes; that is, they had been cleansed from their sin, born again, and had entered the Lord's rest. The four gospels and other writings had been completed, with all the information about the life of Christ. To review these events was not in the scope of the book of Revelation. Also, the world—that is, Rome—would have known about whom he was writing.

And here is the mind which hath wisdom. The seven heads are seven mountains, on which the woman sitteth. And **there are seven kings: five are fallen, and one is,** and the other is not yet come; and when he cometh, he must continue a short space. And the beast that was, and is not, even he is the eighth, and is of the seven, and goeth into perdition. (Revelation 17:9–11 KJV)

The fifth period began at the birth of Christ. It ended at Pentecost. The number fifty is a complete number; that is, ten (the multiple tasks of the cleansing of our Lord) times the fifth period of time is fifty. Pentecost was fifty days from resurrection Sunday. While writing the book of Revelation, John said—in regard to the seven kings of the seven periods—that five had fallen; that is, five were history at that point. The sixth had begun. The dominant kingdom was still Rome during the fifth period and at the beginning of the sixth. Another reason to place the end of the fifth at Pentecost is that John began the sixth seal by recounting the tribulation that began at Pentecost and then gave a judicial symbolic accounting of the chosen saved that happened on the Day of Atonement, which was the same day as Pentecost. Every one of the elect, from the fall of Adam to the last person born again, was included in that accounting. When reading the book of Revelation, keep in mind that John fully understood this. The atonement for sin was provided by Jesus through the cross, and then that atonement became a reality to the chosen saved and was acknowledged in heaven at Pentecost.

The sixth seal recaps the beginning and helps unveil the remainder of the sixth of the seven periods: Revelation 6:2–7:17.

> And <u>I beheld when he had opened the sixth seal</u>, and, lo, there was a great earthquake; and the sun became black as sackcloth of hair, and **the moon became as blood**; And the stars of heaven fell unto the earth, even as a fig tree casteth her untimely figs, when she is shaken of a mighty wind. And the heaven departed as a scroll when it is rolled together; and every mountain and island were moved out of their places. And the kings of the earth, and the great men, and the rich men, and the chief captains, and the mighty men, and every bondman, and every free man, **hid themselves in the dens and in the rocks of the mountains**; And said to the mountains and rocks, Fall on us, and hide us from the face of him that sitteth on the throne,

and from the wrath of the Lamb: For the great day of his wrath is come; and who shall be able to stand? (Revelation 6:12–17 KJV)

And after these things **I saw four angels standing on the four corners of the earth, holding the four winds of the earth**, that the wind should not blow on the earth, nor on the sea, nor on any tree. And I saw another angel ascending from the east, having the seal of the living God: and he cried with a loud voice to the four angels, to whom it was given to hurt the earth and the sea, Saying, Hurt not the earth, neither the sea, nor the trees, **till we have sealed the servants of our God in their foreheads**. And I heard the number of them which were sealed: and there were sealed **an hundred and forty and four thousand of all the tribes of the children of Israel**. Of the tribe of Juda were sealed twelve thousand. Of the tribe of Reuben were sealed twelve thousand. Of the tribe of Gad were sealed twelve thousand. Of the tribe of Aser were sealed twelve thousand. Of the tribe of Nepthali were sealed twelve thousand. Of the tribe of Manasses were sealed twelve thousand. Of the tribe of Simeon were sealed twelve thousand. Of the tribe of Levi were sealed twelve thousand. Of the tribe of Issachar were sealed twelve thousand. Of the tribe of Zabulon were sealed twelve thousand. Of the tribe of Joseph were sealed twelve thousand. Of the tribe of Benjamin were sealed twelve thousand. (Revelation 7:1–8 KJV)

"the moon became as blood": Three words or phrases appear together in the same verse in the Joel 2. They are moon, blood, and last days. Right at or after the events of Pentecost, there were those who didn't understand what was happening. Peter reminded them of Joel's prophecy in Acts 2. Peter quoted the Scripture from Joel, which included those same three words. Peter told them that they were experiencing the fulfillment of Joel's prophecy. Yes, the phrase "last days" began at Pentecost in these Scriptures. John began his writing about the sixth seal with some of the same words and phrases of dramatic events that Joel and Peter had used. John did include "blood" and "moon," but he did not include the phrase "last days." John knew that the church would know about this fulfillment of Joel's prophecy and when it happened. The church would have known that this prophecy was fulfilled. These words were simply used to let the reader know that the sixth seal began at Pentecost. Joel's prophecy was fulfilled on the cross when the Lord's blood was shed for the sin of all who choose to be cleansed. The sign of the moon for the church was the lunar sign of ten times three, or the cleansing the church could now receive. The thirty-day month was the primary sign of the lunar calendar for mankind.

"hid themselves in the dens and in the rocks of the mountains": Pentecost resulted in conflict between the righteous and unrighteous. The destiny of the chosen saved was secured through the Day of Atonement at Pentecost. The destiny of those whose names were not written in the Book of Life was also fixed for eternity. John uses some very dramatic violent language to describe the fate of the lost, which was fixed at the Day of Atonement and will also be experienced after the chosen saved have been taken to be with the Lord.

"I saw four angels standing on the four corners of the earth, holding the four winds of the earth": Watch later in Revelation 9:14 for what happens when these four angels are given permission to release these winds. The Christian has authority over Satan, as he is restricted as to what he can do until the Lord finishes saving the lost. Once again, John communicates to the chosen saved at that time that it will be a while before judgment comes on those who have been persecuting the chosen saved. Satan has been bound, as the Scriptures make it quite clear that he must leave if commanded to do so in the name of Christ. Choose the Lord, and Satan cannot dominate your life. He is bound spiritually.

"till we have sealed the servants of our God in their foreheads": John once again uses an expression from the Old Testament Scriptures; that is, "foreheads."

> And the LORD said to him, "Go through the midst of the city, even through the midst of Jerusalem, and put a mark on the **foreheads of the men** who sigh and groan over all the abominations which are being committed in its midst." (Ezekiel 9:4)

When John uses this expression, he is not talking about a physical mark, the mark that determines the redeemed is the presence of the Holy Spirit indwelling that person.

"an hundred and forty and four thousand of all the tribes of the children of Israel": John did not begin the use of the number one thousand and twelve thousand in the Scriptures. He simply drew once again from what had already been established to express the accounting of the chosen saved at Pentecost. Read another Scripture from the Old Testament that introduces these numbers.

> Of every tribe a thousand, throughout all the tribes of Israel, shall ye send to the war. 5 So there were

delivered out of the thousands of Israel, <u>a thousand of</u> <u>every tribe</u>, twelve thousand armed for war. (Numbers 31:4–5 KJV)

Ten, the multiple tasks of the cleansing work of Jesus, times ten times ten, consistently throughout the Scriptures, suggests that it is finished. Twelve, the witness of Israel, times one thousand then becomes the total number from that witness. Twelve times twelve thousand reinforces that finished number. Jesus did this with the number seventy. How many times should one forgive? Jesus said seventy (ten times seven) times seven. He did not mean 490. Then Jesus compared His kingdom with the debt of one owing ten thousand talents; that is, the sin debt is ten the multiple. The multiple cleansing tasks of Jesus are expressed as ten times a thousand, with the finished number completing the cleansing work.

Remember that the first accounting of the chosen saved after crossing the Red Sea, a type of Pentecost, was taken of the chosen Israel fifty-two Sabbath days after they set foot in the wilderness. The accounting of the chosen Israel was a type of the accounting of the chosen saved at Pentecost—the use of the number twelve thousand and again the number 144, which John will use later in the book of Revelation to totally sum up the number of all the chosen saved in the following Scripture:

After this I beheld, and, lo, a great multitude, which no man could number, of all nations, and kindreds, and people, and tongues, stood before the throne, and before the Lamb, clothed with white robes, and palms in their hands; And cried with a loud voice, saying, Salvation to our God which sitteth upon the throne, and unto the Lamb. And all the angels stood round about the throne, and about the elders and the four beasts, and fell before the throne on their faces, and worshipped God, Saying, Amen: Blessing, and glory, and wisdom, and thanksgiving, and honour, and power, and might, be unto our God for ever and ever. Amen. And one of the elders answered, saying unto me, What are **these which are arrayed in white robes**? and whence came they? And I said unto him, Sir, thou knowest. And he said to me, These are they which came out of great tribulation, and have washed their robes, and made them white in the blood of the Lamb. Therefore are they before the throne of God, and serve him day and night in his temple: and **he that sitteth on the throne shall dwell among them**. They shall hunger no more, neither thirst any more; neither shall the sun light on them, nor any heat. **For the Lamb which is in the midst of the throne shall feed them, and shall lead them** unto living fountains of waters: and God shall wipe away all tears from their eyes. (Revelation 7:9–17 KJV)

"After this I beheld, and, lo, a great multitude": Salvation became the judicial experience of all the redeemed from sin at Pentecost. The redeemed can now say, "I have been saved, I am being saved, and I will be saved at the return of the Lord." All those who had established a faith relationship with the Lord before the Lord called Abraham, all those during the period of the witness of Israel, and all those during the church age were returned to the Lord at the harvest of Pentecost. Remember that the witness spiritually of the chosen saved of Israel and the witness of the chosen saved of the New Testament church became one at Pentecost, through the sacrifice of the Lord Jesus Christ.

"these which are arrayed in white robes": These are all those cleansed from sin. John remembers that they were carrying palm branches. Israel used palm branches to form the booths to live in during the Feast of the Booths. The church is full of the branches that have been folded in to the kingdom of our Lord.

"he that sitteth on the throne shall dwell among them": The fulfillment of the tabernacle experience of Israel has come to pass in the New Testament church. The Lord has taken up residence in the bodies of all the redeemed.

"For the Lamb which is in the midst of the throne shall feed them, and shall lead them": The Lord will lead and guide the redeemed as they serve Him in His kingdom. The Lord would that all the redeemed will chose to enter His abundant life and experience His living waters, entering into the seventh-day rest by faith.

Another Scripture that uses twelve and one thousand to communicate spiritual things:

> And the city lieth **foursquare,** and the length is as large as the breadth: and he measured the city with the reed, **twelve thousand furlongs**. The length and the breadth and the height of it are equal. And he measured the wall thereof, **an hundred and forty and four cubits**, according to the measure of a man, **that is, of the angel**. (Revelation 21:16–17 KJV)

"foursquare": The term was used to describe the organization of the chosen around the tabernacle, which became, at the fulfillment of the sign of the tabernacle, the organization of the church. A square, however, is not described as 12,000 x 12,000 x 12,000.

"twelve thousand furlongs": Twelve thousand simply calls attention to the finished number that will be in that place. The city was a type of the place of the chosen saved that the Lord has prepared for the chosen saved. The number twelve thousand here would not refer to Israel but to the twelve sons of Jacob as the sign of all three periods of the witnesses was organized under those two marriages.

The Holy City was and is a type of that dwelling place. The seventy weeks of Daniel began at the decree that allowed the rebuilding the walls that took fifty-two days to complete. The Lord did establish that destination, the place He has prepared, for the chosen saved at Pentecost.

"an hundred and forty and four cubits": Twelve times twelve is a complete number of the two witnesses.

"that is, of the angel": There are measurements by man, and then there are measurements of the angels. The measurements were given in great detail for the construction of the tabernacle and the temples. It will be interesting to understand how many of these have spiritual meanings that the angels would know. The Lord, through John, identifies these numbers and relates them to God's redemption plan by the phrase, "that is, of the angel." Remember that the Lord gave extensive dimensions that resulted in the tabernacle and Solomon's temple being built physically, as a sign of the spiritual. Ezekiel's temple was organized with multiple chapters of dimensions as a sign of the spiritual dimension of the second temple. Ezekiel's temple began at Pentecost, and the Lord will continue to build it until He returns. Remember that the sign of the eighth day, which was given to the New Testament church, is at the center of the cleansing sign in Ezekiel's temple. There were eight cleansing bowls in Ezekiel's temple.

The sixth seal—that is, the sixth period—began at Pentecost. The sign of Israel is the only benchmark that this writer can reference of when the sixth period ended and the church entered the seventh period. The first council[3] of Israel, which was formed August 29, 1897, in Basle, Switzerland, is probably when this transition occurred. This council included Jews from all over the world. The sign of the chosen Israel tells us more than anything else about the season of the Lord's return. That first council or congress began a series of events that ended in 1948, which systematically accomplished the return of Israel as a nation back to the Holy Land.

The Lord called Theodore Herzl and instilled the idea in his heart to organize Israel to form a nation once again. He discovered that no one where he lived would support that idea. The Lord, however, made him aware of those who did like the idea. Praise the Lord. His way prevailed. Herzl was a dynamic organizer, so when he died after eight years in the work, they were afraid that the work would come to an end, but it wasn't about Herzl. The Lord, in effect, gave us a sign of the eighth day being the goal of this work.

The faithfulness of Israel to accomplish the work that God began through all the tribulation and divisions of that time is simply remarkable. Remember that the approximately eighteen million Jews in the world were reduced by some six million during the four trumpets of the seventh period. Satan certainly responded to these events, knowing that his days were drawing short. The sign of Israel becomes more compelling, as God made it possible that their return would be accomplished.

Adding to the sign was the <u>sixth-day war</u>, which became another sign, as the Holy City is at the center of the fulfillment of the prophecy of the seventieth week of Daniel. Israel is back in the entire Holy City, which fulfills the sign of Israel before the second coming of our Lord. The third of the three sixes will come to a close when the seventh trumpet of the seventh seal. The state of being of the sixth day of mankind will be no more. Six is the state of being of the lost. Three sixes were used to end the three periods of the witness to God's redemption plan. Three sixes simply mean separation from God for eternity. The Lord will return at the end of the third six. The number of the beast in Revelation 13:14 is "six hundred threescore and six." John used numbers from the Old Testament Scriptures to let the reader know that when the lawless one comes, the final or third six is drawing near. The first six was at the end of the first period of the witness.

Ten, the multiple cleansing of the Lord, times ten is one hundred, or a complete number. The faith relationship with the Lord, established by the redeemed, could have known that their sins would be cleansed. The finished cleansing work on the cross was shown by ten times ten times ten. That finished work and the two witnesses are in the three twenties. The last or the third six simply means that the opportunity to be saved will be gone forever. The number begins with a six and ends with a six. The middle six is surrounded by the numerical signs that redemption was available but not accepted.

Prophecies point to certain kingdoms that will be fulfilled in these final conflicts. There are those whom the Lord has called to understand the history of the world kingdoms and who can help the church understand the meaning of what is happening in the world. This writer has read these Scriptures on more than one occasion but does not have enough insight and knowledge to comment on them. There are, however, general observations as to the nature of the conflicts in the last tribulation period.

The seventh seal unseals or unveils the seven divisions of the final seventh period. These seven divisions of time are prophecies of details that reestablish the sign of Israel; that is, the reorganization of Israel as a nation and placing them back in the Holy City. The Holy City is the sign of the place that the Lord has prepared for the redeemed, which they will enter at His second coming.

This section of Scripture is not focused on the events of the seventh trumpet after the Lord returned for the redeemed.

> And when he had opened the seventh seal, there was silence in heaven about the space of half an hour. And I saw the seven angels which stood before God; and to them were given **seven trumpets**. And another angel came and stood at the altar, having a golden censer; and there was given unto him much incense, that he should offer it **with the prayers of all saints** upon the golden altar which was before the throne. And the smoke of the incense, which came with the prayers of the saints, ascended up before God out of the angel's hand. And the angel took the censer, and filled it with fire of the altar, and cast it into the earth: and there were voices, and thunderings, and lightnings, and an earthquake. **And the seven angels which had**

the seven trumpets prepared themselves to sound. The **first** angel sounded, and there followed hail and fire mingled with blood, and they were cast upon the earth: and the <u>third</u> part of trees was burnt up, and all green grass was burnt up. And the **second** angel sounded, and as it were a great mountain burning with fire was cast into the sea: and the <u>third</u> part of the sea became blood; And the <u>third</u> part of the creatures which were in the sea, and had life, died; and the <u>third</u> part of the ships were destroyed. And the **third** angel sounded, and there fell a great star from heaven, burning as it were a lamp, and it fell upon the <u>third</u> part of the rivers, and upon the fountains of waters; And the name of the star is called Wormwood: and the <u>third</u> part of the waters became wormwood; and many men died of the waters, because they were made bitter. And the **fourth** angel sounded, and the <u>third</u> part of the sun was smitten, and the <u>third</u> part of the moon, and the <u>third</u> part of the stars; so as the <u>third</u> part of them was darkened, and the day shone not for a <u>third</u> part of it, and the night likewise. (Revelation 8:1–12 KJV)

"**seven trumpets**": Remember that the priests of the generation of Joshua blew the seven trumpets seven times. The seventh time they blew the trumpets began the cleansing of the Holy Land. John has divided the seventh seal into seven trumpets; that is, periods of time that will end with the seventh trumpet, beginning the cleansing of this world of all sin. The redeemed will be taken out, and God's judgment of the world will begin.

"with the prayers of all saints": Remember the question of how long it will be until the Lord's return? The Lord has heard all the prayers, and they will be answered. The angels took action on the prayers, and the Lord, though John, is about to give some information on when it will be.

"And the seven angels which had the seven trumpets prepared themselves to sound": Then the first four angels sounded their trumpets.

A short review of the first four divisions of the seventh period:

1. They are brief accounts of these four divisions of time.
2. John uses language indicating they contained major conflicts.
3. They are treated as simple birth pangs before getting to the details of the season of the Lord's return and then warning of the judgment to come.
4. John does not seem to communicate that there is a connection or any kind of common purpose.
5. The Holocaust appears to have happened before the end of the events of the fourth trumpet. The third that keeps showing up in this passage of Scripture may have been fulfilled during the Holocaust. Keep in mind that these Scriptures were never intended to be interpreted literally.

> And I beheld, and heard an angel flying through the midst of heaven, saying with a loud voice, **Woe, woe, woe**, to the inhabiters of the earth by reason of the other voices of the trumpet of the three angels, which are yet to sound! (Revelation 8:13 KJV)

The first "woe" ends at the end of the events of the fifth trumpet or the end of the fifth division of time. The second "woe" will end when the events of the sixth trumpet are finished. The third woe begins at the blowing of the seventh trumpet, but this Scripture does not say when it ends. It seems to be implied that it will end when God's judgment on the earth is complete. The term "woe" is used 111 times in the Scriptures. In every case, it describes a circumstance out of God's will and about to suffer the consequences. The three woes connect the last three divisions of time of the seventh period.

The Nature of the Tribulation Changes as John Presents the Last Three Trumpets, as They Have Something in Common

And the fifth angel sounded, and I saw a star fall from heaven unto the earth: and to him was given the key of the bottomless pit. And he opened the bottomless pit; and there arose a smoke out of the pit, as the smoke of a great furnace; and the sun and the air were darkened by reason of the smoke of the pit. And there came out of the smoke locusts upon the earth: and unto them was given power, as the scorpions of the earth have power. And it was commanded them that they should not hurt the grass of the earth, neither any green thing, neither any tree; but only those men which have not the seal of God in their foreheads. And to them it was given that they should not kill them, but that they should be tormented **five** months: and their torment was as the torment of a scorpion, when he striketh a man. And in those days shall men seek death, and shall not find it; and shall desire to die, and death shall flee from them. And the shapes of the locusts were like unto horses prepared unto battle; and on their heads were as it were crowns like gold, and their faces were as the faces of men. And they had hair as the hair of women, and their teeth were as the teeth of lions. And they had breastplates, as it were breastplates of iron; and the sound of their wings was as the sound of chariots of many horses running to battle. And they had tails like unto scorpions, and there were stings in their tails: and their power was to hurt men **five** months. And they had a king over them, which is the angel of the bottomless pit, whose name in the Hebrew tongue is Abaddon, but in the Greek tongue hath his name Apollyon. **One woe is past**; and, behold, there come two woes more hereafter. (Revelation 9:1–12 KJV)

This fifth division of the seventh period began sometime after Israel was reestablished as a people in the Holy Land and then in the Holy City. It will end when the last three-and-a-half-year tribulation begins. These statements are obviously not based on an exegesis of the words in this passage of Scripture but are based on the sign of Israel. Israel has been reorganized as a people with their own civil government in the Holy City. The sign of Israel is <u>complete</u>. The first of the three woes appears to be the transition from unconnected tribulations in the world to tribulations that have a common purpose, which appear to be set up by the false prophet. John shows that there is a relationship between the false prophet and the lawless one, known as the Antichrist, by bringing them together for the judgment. The target of the lawless one, Matthew 24, is the Christian and Jew. This transition is what sets this tribulation period apart from all the other conflicts in the world. The Lord allowed weapons of mass destruction to be developed, which may have influenced this transition period more than anything else. Satan's not being able to stop Israel from becoming a nation and returning to the Holy Land set the stage for this transition.

Are scorpions with stingers in their tails jet-fighter planes or missiles? It certainly appears that John may have seen weapons of war in his vision that he had a hard time describing. There are conflicts in the world, as the language in these Scriptures suggest. The target of the conflicts appears to be the unsaved, as opposed to Israel and the church, when the sixth trumpet sounds.

Five months are not understood as literal in these Scriptures but may be the key to parallel Scriptures that outline this period. John mentions the five months twice in this passage of Scripture. The fifth trumpet and then the mention of two five-month periods bring to mind the following two times that numbers may help understand this transition period.

The fifth month or year appears in the timeline of the Word of the Lord coming to Ezekiel as to the destruction of Jerusalem during the second captivity. Remember that this word was primarily about the destruction of the Holy City and the first temple and not the second temple, which is involved in the prophecy of the season of the Lord's return. The sign of the two temples, however, has been fulfilled. The temple of the Lord is not a building. The Holy City is still the same and exists as the sign of the dwelling place of the chosen. This sign has not been fulfilled, as the place that the Lord has prepared is yet to come. The following three groups of Scriptures may referring to the five months that John used twice in the previous passage of Scripture. The parallel between the fifth, sixth, and seventh year in Ezekiel's timeline to the fifth, sixth, and seventh division of the seventh period is remarkable.

Israel was about to be taken into captivity, and then the temple and the Holy City would be the target of the captors.

> In the **fifth day of the month**, which was **the fifth year** of king Jehoiachin's captivity, The word of the LORD came expressly unto Ezekiel the priest, the son of Buzi, in the land of the Chaldeans by the river Chebar; and the hand of the LORD was there upon him. (Ezekiel 1:2–3 KJV)

Compare the fifth year with the fifth trumpet. The fifth was a time transition, or getting ready for the event. Ezekiel was warning Israel that judgment was to come and that Israel would go into captivity. The temple would be destroyed as a sign of Jesus's going to the cross. The Holy City, however, is still there. The church is preparing to replace the Holy City with that place that the Lord has prepared. It appears that the church has entered that transition period.

> And it came to pass in the **sixth year, in the sixth month, in the fifth day of the month**, as I sat in mine house, and the elders of Judah sat before me, that the hand of the Lord GOD fell there upon me. Then I beheld, and lo a likeness as the appearance of fire: from the appearance of his loins even downward, fire; and from his loins even upward, as the appearance of brightness, as the colour of amber. (Ezekiel 8:1–2 KJV)

Compare the sixth year with the sixth trumpet. At the end of the events of the sixth trumpet, the Lord will appear once again for His church—three divisions of the witness prophesied through the marriages of Jacob that reentered the Promised Land; three groups taken into captivity at the beginning of the captivity when Solomon's temple was destroyed as a type of the cross. These prophecies are about to be fulfilled at the end of this sixth trumpet.

> And it came to pass in the **seventh year, in the fifth month, the tenth day of the month**, that certain of the elders of Israel came to inquire of the LORD, and sat before me. Then came the word of the LORD unto me, saying, Son of man, speak unto the elders of Israel, and say unto them, Thus saith the Lord GOD; Are ye come to inquire of me? As I live, saith the Lord GOD, **I will not be inquired of by you.** (Ezekiel 20:1–3 KJV)

Compare the seventh year with the seventh trumpet. When that seventh trumpet blows, it will be too late to inquire of the Lord. Ezekiel 20 recaps the events of the first captivity as to the knowledge of the redemption plan that was given to them. The knowledge of the gospel must be accepted and acted upon before the Lord returns, or it will be too late.

There were two fives in the passage. Jesus came at the beginning of the fifth seal/fifth period, with His cleansing work becoming the experience of the church at Pentecost, which ended the fifth period (10 x 5, or 50). The first five resulted with the cross on the sixth day and then the first or spiritual resurrection of the redeemed. The second five begins that period that will bring about the return of our

Lord at the end of the sixth trumpet with the bodily resurrection of all the redeemed.

They were only to hurt mankind in the fifth trumpet, and then it changes to slaying people in the events of the sixth trumpet. The nature of the tribulation will change and become more serious for the Christian and Jew when the events of the sixth trumpet come to pass. Praise the Lord that He has promised to take the church out of this world to be with Him before the tribulation intensifies to the judgment on this earth.

The events of the fifth trumpet are the transition period, for whatever length of time, from the unorganized or uncoordinated conflicts to a tribulation period organized with a common purpose directed at the Jew and Christian. Keep in mind that freedom only comes from the Lord. The Lord's influence has created what is known as the free world, which is perceived to be the same as the Christian and Jew.

The Second Three and One-Half Years

The second three and one-half years will end for the church with the second advent of the Lord.

> **And the sixth angel sounded**, and I heard a voice from the four horns of the golden altar which is before God, Saying to the sixth angel which had the trumpet, **Loose the four angels** which are bound in the great river Euphrates. And the four angels were loosed, which were prepared for an hour, and a day, and a month, and a year, for to slay the third part of men. And the number of the army of the horsemen were

two hundred thousand thousand: and I heard the number of them (Revelation 9:13–16 KJV)

Neither repented they of their murders, nor of their sorceries, nor of their fornication, nor of their thefts. (Revelation 9:1 KJV)

"**Loose the four angels**": Satan released after being bound for one thousand years as the end of the church age draws to the end. Keep in mind that the redeemed have been given power over Satan. That power appears to be partially suspended during the last three and one half years. The Word will continue to be preached throughout this period. The slaying of one-third of the Jews was not the fulfillment of Revelation 9:15 but may have been a type of the intensity of this tribulation time that would fulfill this prophecy.

"**two hundred thousand thousand**": One of the problems with numbers is that the translators change them to the current understanding of quantitative values. Read the King James Version of this number, which does not change the number from the original text; the meaning of this number has not changed: " two hundred thousand thousand." The two witnesses are the target of the conflict. The conflict is getting worse. One hundred, a complete number, and then one thousand, a finished number, based on the multiple number ten, the multiple tasks or cleansings of the Lord, and then a thousand times a thousand, making sure one understands that the final conflict is about to be finished. Who will start this war? One thing from the Scriptures that seems clear is that they will come from the East. The lawless one should be recognized during this period.

"**they did not repent of their murders nor of their sorceries nor of their immorality nor of their thefts**": The lack of repentance by the vast majority is the reason for the season of the Lord's return to become a reality.

> And there was given me a reed like unto a rod: and the angel stood, saying, **Rise, and measure the temple of God**, and the altar, and them that worship therein. But the court which is without the temple leave out, and measure it not; for it is given unto the Gentiles: and the holy city shall **they tread under foot forty and two months**. And I will give power unto my two witnesses, and they shall prophesy a_ thousand two hundred and threescore days, clothed in sackcloth. **These are the two olive trees**, and the two candlesticks standing before the God of the earth. (Revelation 11:1–4 KJV)

"Rise, and measure the temple of God": The number of saints written in the Lamb's Book of Life is about to be completed. The courts outside the temple are no longer relevant, as the redeemed have experienced the first spiritual resurrection, as prophesied by their presence in the Holy Place of the second temple.

"they tread under foot forty and two months": Israel and the free world will be the target of the final conflict. The only ones free from the captivity of sin are those that the Messiah has set free. Freedom in the world only becomes available when people repent.

"These are the two olive trees": The two olive trees or olive branches were in the second temple. John references these to make sure that readers would understand that the two witnesses are Israel and the church. They were placed in the holy place within the second temple.

The Second Coming of the Lord at the Last Trumpet

And after the three and a half days the breath of life from God came into them, and they stood on their feet; and great fear fell upon those who were beholding them. **And they heard a loud voice from heaven saying to them, "Come up here**." And they went up into heaven in the cloud, and their enemies beheld them. And in that hour there was a great earthquake, and a tenth of the city fell; and seven thousand people were killed in the earthquake, and the rest were terrified and gave glory to the God of heaven. **The second woe is past; behold, the third woe** is coming quickly. Then the **seventh angel sounded**; and there were loud voices in heaven, saying, " **The kingdom of the world has become the kingdom of our Lord and of His Christ; and He will reign forever and ever."** And the twenty-four elders, who sit on their thrones before God, fell on their faces and worshiped God, saying, "We give You thanks, O Lord God, the Almighty, who are and who were, because You have taken Your great power and have begun to reign. "And the nations were enraged, and Your wrath came, **and the time came for the <u>dead</u> to be judged, and the time to reward Your bond-servants the prophets and the saints** and those who fear Your name, the small and the great, and to destroy those who destroy the earth." (Revelation 11:11–18 NASB)

"And after the three and a half days the breath of life from God came into them": The resurrection of the bodies of the redeemed will be complete at the end of the three-and-one-half-year period.

"And they heard a loud voice from heaven saying to them, "Come up here": Remember, the Lord will return with a shout. Where is "here" located? Paradise? Where is that? Heaven? Where is that? How many books have been written trying to define these locations? It is where the Lord will be. What else does one need to know? Knowledge of sin and its presence will not be there, which is probably worth mentioning.

"The second woe is past; behold, the third woe": The second of the three woes that help unify the events of the last three trumpets ends at the second coming of the Lord.

"the seventh angel sounded": Good news for the redeemed but a death sentence for all those who have never acknowledged the Savior as Lord of their lives. Jesus said you must be born again. The Lord just sent chills up and down my spine when this section of Scripture was read.

"The kingdom of the world has become the kingdom of our Lord and of His Christ; and He will reign forever and ever": The kingdom becomes literal for the saints. The saints will know the rest of the story. Temptation will be no more. The redeemed will enter that place the Lord has prepared for them. It will be a perfect place, no matter whether it is in this world made new or another place. The Scripture says that there will be no need for the sun, as Jesus will be the light.

"and the time came for the dead to be judged, and the time to reward Your bond-servants the prophets and the saints": The judgment has come for the lost and the redeemed. The final conflict will cleanse this earth. The generation of Joshua cleansed the Holy

Land when they went in after they crossed the Jordan as a type of this end-time cleansing. This end-time cleansing will happen after the church has crossed the Jordan; that is, has been taken up by the Lord.

All the chosen saved will enter that place that the Lord has prepared. John speaks of a new heaven and a new earth. This writer simply has no insight as to whether this is a literal new earth or this earth renewed.

Additional Information about the Lawless One and Those Who Will Join Him, Causing the Last Three-and-One-Half-Year Tribulation Period

And then shall that Wicked be revealed, whom the Lord shall consume with the spirit of his mouth, and **shall destroy with the brightness of his coming**: Even him, whose coming is after the working of Satan with all power and signs and lying wonders. (2 Thessalonians 2:8–9 KJV)

The Lord is coming for His church, but He is also coming to judge the world. The judgment of this world will begin at the blowing of the seventh trumpet of the seventh seal of Revelation, with the purging of this world by the seven events of the bowls of wrath, and will end with the final judgment.

And here is the mind which hath wisdom. The seven heads are seven mountains, on which the woman sitteth. And there are seven kings: five are fallen, and one is, **and the other is not yet come; and when he cometh, he must continue a short space. And the**

beast that was, and is not, even he is the eighth, and is of the seven, and **goeth into perdition. And the ten horns which thou sawest are ten kings**, which have received no kingdom as yet; **but receive power as kings one hour with the beast**. These have one mind, and shall give their power and strength unto the beast. These shall make war with the Lamb, and the Lamb shall overcome them: for he is Lord of lords, and King of kings: and they that are with him are called, and chosen, and faithful. And he saith unto me, The waters which thou sawest, where the whore sitteth, are peoples, and multitudes, and nations, and tongues. And the ten horns which thou sawest upon the beast, these shall hate the whore, and **shall make her desolate** and naked, and shall eat her flesh, and burn her with fire. For God **hath put in their hearts to fulfil his will, and to agree, and give their kingdom unto the beast**, until the words of God shall be fulfilled. And the woman which thou sawest **is that great city**, which reigneth over the kings of the earth. (Revelation 17:9–18 KJV)

"and the other is not yet come; and when he cometh, he must continue a short space": The kingdoms of this world that exist in the last division of the seventh period will not reign long. This may be the seven years of which Ezekiel spoke.

"And the beast which was and is not": In Revelation 13, John recaps the first beast—that is, the beast from the sea—and then presents the beast of the earth that will come at the end time. Remember that the fourth beast was Rome, but the one that destroyed the second temple is the one referred to here as "the beast which was and is not." The Scripture separated this one out of Rome so that these end-time Scriptures would not be confused with Rome. In Revelation 17, John brings these two together to show the relationship of the two. Remember that Jesus did this in Matthew 24. The destruction of the temple was a type of the end-time destruction at His second coming. The beast of the past was Titus.

"**even he is the eighth, and is of the seven**": The type becomes the one at the final event, the beast of the earth. He is to be one of the seven; that is, one in the seventh period of time. He is also an eighth, as he will continue to exist after the church has entered the eighth-day period. It is thought that the lawless one will become known in the events of the sixth trumpet.

"**goeth into perdition**": The lawless one will be destroyed in the last conflict; that is, the events that begin with the sound of the last or seventh trumpet.

"**And the ten horns which you saw are ten kings**": These ten kings were yet to come when John was writing this Scripture. Once again, ten, as the multiple number, is more than likely the total number of countries that respond to the lawless one. It could be ten countries, but it would probably not be wise to try counting them.

"**but receive power as kings one hour with the beast**": These have one purpose. That one purpose is powerful enough to bring them all together to follow the beast of the earth. One hour that lasts for three and a half years yet is a short time.

"**shall make her desolate**": It will be interesting to learn how much of the desolation that these kings have caused is spiritual and how much is physical. The spiritual desolation is, of course, what will become an abomination to the Lord that brings about the final destruction. The harlot is all the kingdoms of this world. The righteousness of God will not be found in the vast majority of the people. Spiritual desolation will be the state of being of mankind.

"hath put in their hearts to fulfil his will, and to agree, and give their kingdom unto the beast": Those who join the lawless one have sold out to the common purpose that joins them with the lawless one, in spite of differences they may have.

"is that great city": The Holy City has been the center of the witness of God's redemption plan since it was established through the calling of Abraham. The beast and his followers set out to destroy all of the witnesses to God's redemption plan, trying to purge the world from all the freedom and righteousness that God has provided, only to end up being defeated and causing the entire world to be destroyed. Satan is a liar, and his prophets have been spreading his lies. How long have the prophecies of God through John been before the world, yet the world has chosen to believe the lies of Satan?

A Second Account of the Second Coming of the Lord, Revealing That He Also Has Come to Judge the World

And I saw heaven opened, and behold a white horse; and he that sat upon him was called Faithful and True, and in righteousness **he doth judge and make war**. His eyes were as a flame of fire, and on his head were many crowns; and he had a name written, that no man knew, but he himself. And he was clothed with a vesture dipped in blood: and his name is called The Word of God. And the armies which were in heaven followed him upon white horses, clothed in fine linen, white and clean. And out of his mouth goeth a sharp sword, that with it he should smite the nations: and he shall rule them with a rod of iron: and he treadeth the winepress of the fierceness and wrath of Almighty God. And he hath on his vesture and on his thigh a name written, KING OF KINGS, AND LORD OF LORDS. (Revelation 19:11–16 KJV)

And the beast was taken, and with him the false prophet that wrought miracles before him, with which he deceived them that had received the mark of the beast, and them that worshipped his image. These both were cast alive into a lake of fire burning with brimstone. (Revelation 19:20 KJV)

And the devil that deceived them was cast into the lake of fire and brimstone, where the beast and the false prophet are, and shall be tormented day and night for ever and ever. (Revelation 20:10 KJV)

"**he doth judge and make war**": I doubt that drone warfare will work in this case.

"**And the beast was taken, and with him the false prophet**": John includes the message of the false prophet in the divisions of the judgment on this world. Who is this false prophet, and where and when did he prophesy? When did these people receive the mark of the beast? The Scriptures often speak of false prophets, but only this one appears to have a relationship with the lawless one. Keep in mind that many or millions are deceived by this prophet. That surely would take a lot of time. The <u>words</u> of the false prophet are presented in the Revelation 16 as being involved in the purging of this world, and then the false prophet and the lawless one are brought together for the last judgment. John has shown us that there is a relationship between the two, even if they did not live at the same time.

"And the devil that deceived them was cast into the lake of fire and brimstone, where the beast and the false prophet are": Yes, Satan will have deceived the beast and false prophet.

> He which testifieth these things saith, **Surely I come quickly**. Amen. Even so, **come, Lord Jesus.** (Revelation 22:20 KJV)

"Surely I come quickly": John brought his writing in the book of Revelation to a close with these words from the Lord. Remember that the primary thing that the Lord unveiled through John is information about the season of His return and the judgment after His return. John has included references to the gospel and the history of the prophecy and organization of the gospel in the book of Revelation, which already had been given through previous Scriptures. The season of the Lord's return was on John's mind when he finished writing the book.

"Come Lord Jesus": The chosen saved join with John's response to say, "Come, Lord Jesus." A faith relationship with the Lord resulting in being born again is the only way that one will be ready for that day. Remember—only God the Father knows the day and hour of the return of Jesus.

> And they that be wise shall shine as the brightness of the firmament; and they that turn many to righteousness as the stars for ever and ever. (Daniel 12:3)

This chapter began with a passage of Scriptures from Daniel 12 that contained this verse. The last three and a half days are a lot closer now than when Daniel wrote these words, but it seems that it would still be wise to proclaim His righteousness to as many as we can.

Okay, go ahead and play all the keys, black and white, and you will have played eighty-eight keys. Ten times eight plus eight. Could it be that the last eight have arrived, representing the eighth Sabbath rest that we all look forward to experiencing?

1   *Biblesoft's New Exhaustive Strong's Numbers and Concordance with Expanded Greek-Hebrew Dictionary* (Biblesoft and International Bible Translators, Inc., 1994).
2   *The New Unger's Bible Dictionary* (Chicago: Moody Press, 1988).
3   Solomon Grayzel, *A History of the Jews* (Philadelphia: Jewish Publication Society of America, 1977).